# JULIAN'S WAY

# JULIAN'S WAY

## A PRACTICAL COMMENTARY
## ON JULIAN OF NORWICH

*Ritamary Bradley*

HarperCollins*Religious*
*An imprint of* HarperCollins*Publishers*

HarperCollins*Religious*
Part of HarperCollins*Publishers*
77–85 Fulham Palace Road, London W6 8JB

First published in Great Britain
in 1992 by HarperCollins*Religious*

1 3 5 7 9 10 8 6 4 2

A catalogue record for this book is
available from the British Library

ISBN 0 00 599275-3

Printed and bound in Great Britain by
HarperCollinsManufacturing Glasgow

Scripture selections are taken from the **New American Bible With
Revised New Testament** Copyright © 1986 by the Confraternity of
Christian Doctrine, Washington, D.C. and are used with permission.
All rights reserved.

We thank the publishers for permission to use the following materials:

"Millet's 'Feeding Her Birds'" from *Selected Poetry of Jessica Powers*, ed.
Regina Siegfried and Robert Morneau (Kansas City: Sheed and Ward,
© 1989).

Selections from Jeffrey F. Hamburger, *Art and Mysticism in Flanders and
the Rhineland circa 1300* (New Haven and London: Yale University Press,
© 1990).

Lines from Denise Levertov's "On a Theme from Julian's Chapter XX",
*Breathing the Water* (New York: New Directions Publishing Corporation,
© 1987).

"It is plain that mysticism, like other subjects, may arouse either a practical or a theoretical interest. *The practical interest is that of the one who aspires to tread the mystic path.* The theoretical interest, whether in mysticism or anything else, is that of the one who simply desires to know, and who values knowledge for its own sake." W. T. Stace, *Mysticism and Philosophy*, New York, The Macmillan Press, 1971, 19.

# CONTENTS

## Contents

# ACKNOWLEDGEMENTS

I wish to thank all those who have shared with me their understandings of Julian. In particular, I should like to mention Marion Glasscoe, Valerie Lagorio and many others associated with *Mystics Quarterly*; John Clark; Brant Pelphrey; and the Friends of the Julian Shrine in Norwich. To Saint Ambrose University I owe thanks for assistance in preparing the manuscript.

# PREFACE

The *Showings* of Julian of Norwich is becoming one of the best-known classics on the Christ-life in our times. The treatise is calling forth extensive scholarly, devotional and academic commentary. Dramatic works are drawing their content from the *Showings*. A major poet, Denise Levertov, has enshrined the wisdom of Julian in a series of poems. She captures the core of that wisdom when she writes:

> *The oneing*, she saw, *the oneing*
> *with the Godhead* opened Him utterly
> to the pain of all minds, all bodies
> —sands of the sea, of the desert—
> from first beginning
> to last day.[1]

This book "with reverent drede" dares to join that splendid company of commentators and interpreters. These chapters are addressed to readers already somewhat familiar with the *Showings*. My aim is to reconsider the backgrounds from which Julian's treatise comes, and by reflection and study, to take seriously her own practice of probing ever more deeply into the text. I hope thereby to contribute to the further understanding of Julian's words, in a spirit of love.

Such is Julian's counsel, when she says: "Let every one accept these words as our Lord intended them, according to the grace God gives to each in understanding and love" (LT 26).[2]

The graces we receive also include the insights of our times, from human progress and from Christian wisdom. I have tried to search such contemporary sources while listening to the voice of the original text, without overshadowing the situation from which the original writings come.

To understand Julian properly, we need all the available resources. Since we have very little evidence outside the text about her, a chief resource is the language she uses and the literary form in which she expresses herself.

In this connection we have the caution of the scribe who exhorts us "to beware that you do not take one thing according to your inclination and liking and neglect another ... But take everything with all, and truly understand that all is in accord with Holy Scripture and grounded in the same" (scribal addition to LT 86). But even with the will to follow this directive, we do not find it easy to see the whole of Julian's teaching on any one subject. This book, therefore, undertakes to follow through the entire text on a selection of topics that are touched on again and again by Julian, though not completely in any one part.

Much attention has rightfully been given to the differences between the short and the long texts. But a surer measure of Julian's deepening insight lies within the long text itself. Though all is contained in the first showing, as in an embryo, the meanings unfold in sequence. What she learns intensifies with each new revelation. Furthermore, since the text itself shows evidence of reworking, there is an overlay of insights which reflect a sense of the whole at the same time each showing is taught. Julian's years of counselling, as well as her own contemplative way of life, contribute to this reworking. Hence, the text becomes a plan for life—a way.

Sometimes an interpretation hinges on a choice of readings when there are variants between the manuscripts of the long text, or when it may be helpful to refer back to the short text. Even then, an interpretation is uncertain, inasmuch as the manuscripts do not go back to Julian's own time but date from the seventeenth century.

We have the long texts only because of the "piety and learning of Augustine Baker and his spiritual school among the exiled Benedictine monks and nuns in the Low Countries and France" after the Dissolution of the monasteries.[3] Few books are more simple, yet paradoxically more difficult. Edmund Colledge and James Walsh acknowledge this point in the introduction to their translation of the text. They are commenting on how Julian ranked with other religious writers of her time and on the sparse manuscript tradition which has preserved the *Showings*:

> The manuscript tradition [of the *Showings*] indicates that until the mid-17th century it enjoyed only limited circulation.... If we seek the reason for the comparative lack of popularity of this work, until the Baker school rescued it from oblivion, they are not hard to find. Julian's book is by far the most profound and difficult of all mediaeval spiritual writings. ...[4]

Lacking popular appeal in the Middle Ages, the *Showings* was less widely circulated than the writings of Richard Rolle and his followers. Her book was even less well-known than Walter Hilton's clear, systematic, and somewhat traditional works. The *Cloud* author, too, with his treatises rooted in the approach of Denys the pseudo-Areopagite, surpassed Julian in range of audience.

But times have changed. The popularity of Julian grows apace. In inaugurating their project on the Classics of Western Spirituality, the Paulist Press editors responded to reader interest when they chose the *Showings* as the first in the series.

Centres of contemplative living and study give a central place to the wisdom of the *Showings*. A further impetus for Julian studies springs from her place in women's studies, as she is the first known woman writer of English prose. Because her treatise shows awareness of the feminine, excerpts from the work have begun to appear in literary anthologies for women's studies. Graduate students continue to choose Julian as their dissertation subject.

This book also aims to assist scholars whose graduate programmes and subsequent studies did not include the mystics. It should be of help to those teaching the mystics in universities, colleges, and seminaries. Furthermore, the thematic approach to Julian should illustrate how other mystics can be read and studied. Those who have used *Enfolded in Love*, a gathering of texts from the *Showings*, already attest to the value of the thematic approach for devotional purposes.[5]

This Practical Commentary attempts to speak to such an expanding audience.

At this point we should take note of Julian's own definition of her audience: she writes for the simple and not for the wise, for they must already know these things (LT 9). But Julian's book is not an example of "an edifying literature found more or less everywhere in the hands of all and sundry which, in relation to high theology, is derivative and merely repeats in simplified form what is aready to be found in the theology textbooks of the schools".[6] As Karl Rahner says: "... there is also a literature of spirituality which stands in a different relationship to learned theology and it is not only Holy Scripture and the pronouncements of the Church's magisterium that belong to it. It is a literature of piety which forestalls theological reflection, which is more fundamentally spontaneous than the latter, wiser and more experienced than the wisdom of the learned. ..." It is "a literature in which the Church's belief, the Word of God and the action of the Holy Spirit, which never ceases to be operative in the Church, find more authentic expression than in the treatises of theologians."[7]

Rahner is speaking here of the Spiritual Exercises of St Ignatius of Loyola, but what he says applies very well to the *Showings*. They, too, are "a new gift by God's Spirit of the ancient Christianity to a new age." They are also "for an age that is only just starting." They have "something to say to theology which this cannot otherwise come to know." In approaching them we should not "start with the tacit assumption that in them there cannot be anything more than what theological speculation has dealt with long ago." Above all, one must take care that the teachers in their professorial chairs do not weaken and dilute such literature "until what was at first a great light becomes a candle giving a cozy glow to Everyman's little room".[8]

It is hoped that Julian's great light will burn on for the readers of this Commentary. Insight alone can yield only darkness in the end. Teachers, drawing on scholarship alone, can reduce the light to a cosy glow. It is hoped that by pointing readers to a discreet combining of both insight and scholarship, this Commentary will help Julian's great light to burn on ever brighter.

\* \* \*

This Commentary is supported by quotations and citations from Marion Glasscoe's edition of British Library Sloane Manuscript, No. 2499: *A Revelation of Love* (Exeter: Exeter University Press, 1989) (identified as the Long Text and abbreviated as LT).[9] For the Short Text (abbreviated ST), references are to Frances Beer, *Julian of Norwich's Revelations of Divine*

Love (Heidelberg, Carl Winter, 1978). The manuscript of this edition is BL, Additional Manuscripts No. 33790. Unless otherwise indicated, the translations are my own.

The parenthetical references are included throughout this Commentary to make it easy for the reader to refer to the text, and especially to the context, of Julian's book.

## Endnotes

1. "On a Theme from Julian's Chapter XX", from *Breathing the Water* (New Directions Publishing Company, 1987), Copyright 1987 by Denise Levertov. Reprinted by permission of New Direction Publishing Corporation.
2. See end of Preface for an explanation of abbreviations and texts cited.
3. *Showings Julian of Norwich*, trans. Edmund Colledge and James Walsh. The Classics of Western Spirituality (New York, Paulist Press, 1978) 22.
4. Colledge and Walsh, translation, 21–22.
5. *Enfolded in Love*, ed. Robert Llewelyn (London, Darton, Longman & Todd, 1980).
6. Karl Rahner, *The Dynamic Element in the Church* (New York, Herder and Herder, 1984) 85.
7. Rahner 85.
8. Rahner 85–89.
9. In making this choice we follow such scholars as Sister Anna Maria Reynolds and Marion Glasscoe in their preference for the Sloane manuscript over the Paris manuscript (P.), Bibliothèque Nationale, Fonds Anglais No. 40. (A third extant manuscript, BL Sloane Ms. No. 3705, is a later copy of SI). As Glasscoe says of Sloane I: "Its language is much closer to fourteenth-century English than that of P." Though some of its readings are "awkward," they are not "impossible," and it seems to be "intended as a faithful copy of an earlier version." (Glasscoe viii).

# I

# THE ANONYMOUS
# AUTHOR OF
# THE SHOWINGS

## WHO IS JULIAN? (1342–c. 1420)

Julian of Norwich—or Dame Julian or Lady Julian—speaks
to our time, though she lived in another era, remote from
our memories. She was an anchoress living in pre-Reformation years, in a cell attached to the church of St. Julian's
in Norwich of the county of Norfolk. It is probable that
she was named for the church. A reconstructed form of her
cell is a place of pilgrimage. There is a guest house on the
grounds, which for many years was kept by the Anglican
Sisters of All Hallows, and still serves visitors. Anglican clergy
minister to those who gather for prayer and counsel at St.
Julian's.

Julian speaks through the slight corpus of her writings—two
accounts of her religious experience, versions which overlap
in what they say. We know these writings as her *Showings*,
or as *Revelations of Divine Love*, or, more simply, as *A Revelation of Love*. The short-text has a crisp immediacy. The long-
text is rich with some twenty years of her reflection.[1] The
differences between the two point to the kind of growth
which marked Julian's life in Christ. She retained the memory
of the sixteen showings, and though after 8 May 1373, the

1

date of the visions, she saw no more, the words spoken in her understanding and her spiritual insights continued over the years.

She also speaks through the responses her readers have to these writings, as these readers, whether devotional or scholarly or both, search the depths of her deceptively simple treatises.

Julian has never been declared a saint in the Catholic Church, but she has a feast day in some Benedictine calendars—for example, Corona Sanctorum Anni Benedictine, 1947. The day chosen is 13 May, once thought to have been the day of the visions. The Anglican communion honours her on 8 May.[2]

Why did she write? For our comfort. For whom did she write? For all Christ's lovers, whom she calls her even-Christians. Julian's way is an invitation to all.[3]

We know her mind and spirit well, but, because she wanted it that way, we know little of her particular life circumstances or who she was.

We do know, of course, that she lived in a time of turmoil, felt by the church and society. She lived in England during the reigns of Edward III and Richard II. In those pre-Reformation years, even local churches in Norfolk must have been troubled by the unsettled state in Rome, when at one period (1378–1409) there were two popes, and at another (1409–1414), there were three. Whatever her degree of awareness of such turmoil, she could not have missed the terror evoked by the plague which ravaged England during her lifetime. The Black Death struck Norwich in 1348–49, when Julian was six, killing, it is thought, up to 50,000 persons. It arrived again in 1361, and yet again in 1369, when Julian was twenty-nine.[4]

Linguistic traces in the Middle English in which Julian

wrote led some to speculate that she may have migrated from the North. But these dialect sprinklings may have come from the scribes who copied her treatises. Flemish was widely in use in the city of Norwich and may have influenced the language spoken in that city.

We have only sparse knowledge of Julian's associations with others, but we know she loved her "even-Christians." Her writings reveal that her mother, and also unnamed friends, were at her bedside during the illness which was the occasion of the visions. A priest came, bringing a little child with him. A priest was with her after the night of her temptation, when she was ready to ignore her showings and attribute them to the ravings of a sick person. As an anchoress her contacts with others were limited, but she lived in the midst of activity. "The three windows of the anchorite's cell allowed Julian to look into her chapel where her attendant priest celebrated the eucharist, to see into the living room kitchen where her friends cared for her, and to see out into the world of fourteenth-century Norwich."[5] Margery Kempe was among those who visited her in order to seek help from one who, she says, was renowned for giving good counsel. Julian loved some persons very well, for in her dialogue with Christ she asks how such and such a person fares before God. Her early years, whatever may have been their circumstances, drew praise from God for her travail and service in youth (LT 14).

She tells us a little about what she prayed for before the time of the revelations. First, there were three petitions that emerged from the teachings of the church about Christ's passion and from "the paintings of crucifixes" which were made in accord with such teachings. Already immersed in devotion to Christ's passion, Julian desired to see in realistic images—in a vision—the passion of Christ. She would like to have been at the crucifixion in the company of these who were there, including Mary Magdalene and those others who loved him.

Following the church's teaching on contrition for sin, she felt spontaneously a desire to have an illness which would bring her near to death, at the age of thirty, and would allow her to suffer all the fears and anguish of dying, so that, upon recovering, she might live a holier life. Then when the hour of death did come, she hoped to go speedily to God. But these two gifts she sought only conditionally, only if God so willed.

Lastly, she prayed for deep feelings and searing affections which her devout contemporaries called "wounds." These wounds are contrition, compassion, and longing for God. Her showings—the sixteen revelations—were vivid imaginative portrayals accompanied by interior "stirrings"—that is, thoughtful reflections and spontaneous movements of her spirit. She invites us to share her experience of imagination, as in listening to a story; of reasoning and reflection; and of openness to intuitive insights, which for her included moments of intense mystical awareness.

All we know of Julian's relationship to God is contained in her book. Within that book references to ordinary experiences are also minimal. But she does mention earth and gardening; water, rain, and the sea; herring scales; pieces of cloth hung out to dry; the drying of wood; food and drink; clothing; a purse; a hazelnut; prison; light and darkness; pain and suffering; joy; friendship; music; a banquet; a dying child. These are scarcely enough for us to reconstruct the details of her life, but they bring us close to the reality of her world.

## An Answer to Prayer?

It is important to note that Julian's prayer for the three gifts—contrition, compassion, and union with God—was not answered in the way she seemed to have expected. God taught her something else as a background for receiving these gifts. Though there is an interlocking of her experience of these gifts throughout the treatise, the order of their fulfilment is changed. And what she asked for and what actually transpired differ.

In the first place Julian had made her petitions for the sake of her own greater holiness of life: she saw the near-death experience to be an occasion of purgation ("to be purged by the mercy of God," through the cessation of "the comfort of earthly life"). Because of this sickness she expected to be able "to live more to the honour of God" (LT 2). But she learns progressively that her experience is also for others.

She is cast in the role of teacher. But women did not teach. They were forbidden to do so. And even within the pattern of teaching as practised by men, there seemed no precedent for what she must undertake to do.

Parish priests were charged with instructing their parishioners in the rudiments of faith and Christian morality, chiefly the creed and the commandments. But Julian has something to say beyond these rudiments, though not in conflict with them.

Clerics at the universities taught for the intellect, often more speculatively than practically; or they prepared future priests for their charge. Julian's lessons involve perception and understanding, focused on love.

Monk teachers of monastic theology did indeed instruct in a form of learning that was intended to enrich the lives of their disciples. But the teaching was primarily adapted to the life of faith led in a monastery. Julian has for her audience all "the dear, dear people of God".

Hermits, such as Richard Rolle (c. 1300–1349), and others centred on the solitary life, such as the author of the *Cloud of Unknowing* (late fourteenth century), also adopted a practical approach with an emphasis on love: in fact, they spoke primarily to the heart, discounting the role of intellect as much as possible. But Julian's showings in part are addressed to the understanding, and she is urged to exercise her reason in order to grasp more fully the lesson of love.

Most important of all, even English mystics contemporary with her, and the monk teachers, only reluctantly adapt their lessons to those not separated from the world, in monastery or hermitage. Julian makes no distinction among modes of leading the Christian life in its fullness. There is, therefore, no precise model in her own times for the kind of teacher she becomes.

True, she herself chose the life of a recluse, which was clearly suited to her person and mission. But she does not stress apartness from the world as a necessary norm for living the life of faith and total commitment. In Norwich she was in proximity to many houses of religious of the regular orders,[6] such as the Benedictines of Carrow nearby. Norwich also knew of three houses of beguines, after the model of those of the Netherlands in the twelfth century, sisterhoods not under ecclesiastical control.[7]

But Julian is still left with the dilemma of how to teach what has been revealed to her without setting herself up as a teacher. In fact, her status as a recluse carried with it a further ban against teaching: women were warned in the *Ancrene Riwle* not to be so bold as to attempt to teach the priests who were sent to minister to them.[8] How, then, can she convey her lessons to others without being a teacher?

First, she will not offer to teach the "wise" but only the simple. And to accomplish this, she constructs the rhetorical strategy of her text. She uses the concept of Christ, the teacher, as this rhetorical strategy, portraying herself—not as teacher—but as one of those taught. At the same time she invites the reader also to take the stance of one learning, according to individual capacity, from Christ, the teacher.

## Christ, the Teacher

On a first reading of the *Showings*, we meet the dominant images of Christ as servant, in the Lord and Servant parable, and as mother, in the motherhood chapters. But on further analysis it becomes clear that the most pervasive Christ-image is that of teacher. By her handling of this image:

> ... Julian creates a rhetorical strategy which sets her
> work apart from other writings of its kind. She avoids
> the method of classical wisdom literature, which
> portrays the writer as a guide instructing one or more
> others. Likewise, she circumvents a method widespread
> in vision literature, in which the visionary simply
> reports personal revelations. Instead, she creates a
> dramatic construct built on the relation of disciple to
> teacher. And, in harmony with her basic purpose—to
> write for all Christ's lovers—she creates a second
> rhetorical level, which draws each reader into dialogue
> with Christ, the teacher, with each one learning
> according to personal gifts of reason and grace. Though
> from the beginning Julian perceives a correspondence
> between the teaching roles of Christ and the Church,
> this bond grows stronger in her experience as the
> Showings unfold.[9]

It is in the context of seeing Christ as teacher that Julian affirms her twofold faith in the church and in her revelations. First, as to the church, she says: "God showed the very great pleasure he has in all men and women who, strongly and wisely, accept the preaching and the teaching of holy church, for he is holy church: he is the ground, he is the substance, he is the teaching, he is the taught, and he is the reward (LT 34).

Then, speaking of the revelations: "All this friendly showing of our courteous Lord is a lovely lesson; it is a sweet gracious teaching, and it comes from him, for the comforting of our soul" (LT 79).

Julian, then, is one open to learning, from the church and from her own experience. She welcomes us to the company of those who listen to the one teacher. We listen to her who is especially apt at learning, especially candid about her efforts and setbacks and progress.

Thus we enter upon Julian's way.

## Endnotes

1. Four manuscripts of the *Showings* are extant: a short version, preserved in the British Library, Additional Manuscripts No. 33790 (Amherst); and three copies of the longer version: Sloane manuscripts, No. 2499 and No. 3705 (designated as Sloane I and II), also in the British Library; and in Paris, Bibliothèque Nationale, Fonds Anglais, No. 40. "It is possible that they were all connected with the work of the Benedictines of the counter-reformation who were active in reviving earlier modes of religious life. Augustine Baker, while he was spiritual director of the English Benedictine nuns in exile in Cambrai, wrote to his friend Sir Robert Cotton asking him for copies of the devotional works of the Medieval period." Marion Glasscoe, ed. *A Revelation of Love*, viii.

A printed version dates from 1670: *XVI Revelations of Divine Love, Shewed to a Devout Servant of our Lord, called Mother Juliana an Anchorete of Norwich: Who lived in the Dayes of King Edward the Third*, ed. R.F.S. Cressy (London, 1670).

2. This discrepancy in dates arises from a different reading of the manuscripts. 8 May is widely accepted as the correct date.

3. For a colourful introduction to Julian's life and times, see Sheila Upjohn, *In Search of Julian of Norwich* (London, Darton, Longman and Todd, 1989).

4. Brant Pelphrey, *Love Was His Meaning The Theology and Mysticism of Julian of Norwich*, ed. James Hogg (Salzburg: Universitität Salzburg, 1982) 47. See also John J. Bagley, *Life in Medieval England* (New York, Putnam, 1960) esp. 158 ff.

5. Alan Webster, "Julian of Norwich", in *Julian and her Norwich*, ed. Frank Sayer (Norwich, Julian of Norwich 1973 Celebration Committee, 1973) 30.

6. Those formally approved and regulated by church authority.

7. "Beguines (masc. beghards) were people in communities, devoted to the service of the needy and to contemplation, common in the Netherlands from the 12th century. They did not take vows and were free to leave the community and marry. There were three such sisterhoods known in Norwich." *Julian and her Norwich* 44.

8. *The Ancrene Riwle*, trans. M.B. Salu (Notre Dame, Ind., University of Notre Dame Press, 1956) 28.

9. Ritamary Bradley, "Christ, the Teacher in Julian's *Showings*: the Biblical and Patristic Traditions," in *The Medieval Mystical Tradition in England*, ed. Marion Glasscoe (Exeter, University of Exeter, 1982) 127–8.

# JULIAN AS ANCHORESS

Julian's adherence to the teaching church did not preclude her creative adaptations of the anchoritic traditions to which she was heir.[1] Such adaptations were imperative if she was to carry out the mission of making known to others what Christ the Teacher revealed to her. This becomes clear when we look at what was expected of her as anchoress, how she seemed to have modified this tradition, and why she did so.

## Her Daily Life

Julian as an anchoress promised canonical obedience to the church, but her exact rule of life was not prescribed. If she observed what is laid down in the twelfth-century Rule for Anchoresses (*Ancrene Riwle*) she had a day primarily given to prayer. Here is a probable schedule:

### The Anchoress's Horarium (Winter)

| | |
|---|---|
| 3:30 a.m. | Preliminary prayers and devotions |
| 5:00 | MATINS AND LAUDS OF OUR LADY |
| | Dirige (Matins and Lauds of the Office of the Dead) |
| | Lauds of the Holy Ghost (optional) |
| | Suffrages and Commendations |
| | Prime of the Holy Ghost (optional) |
| | PRIME OF OUR LADY |
| | Pretiosa |
| | Terce of the Holy Ghost (optional) |
| 8:00 | TERCE OF OUR LADY |
| | Litany of the Saints (daily except Sundays) |
| | The Seven Penitential Psalms |
| | The Fifteen Gradual Psalms |
| | Prayers and Supplications |
| | Devotions before the cross |
| | Devotions to Our Lady |

| 11:30 | MASS (Communion fifteen times a year) |
| | Sext of the Holy Ghost (optional) |
| | SEXT OF OUR LADY |
| | None of the Holy Ghost (optional) |
| | NONE OF OUR LADY |
| | Meal with graces (the only meal on ferias in winter) |
| | Rest period |
| 3:00 p.m. | Private prayers and meditation |
| | Reading in the Psalter, (*AR*), and other books in French and English |
| 4:00 | Vespers of the Holy Ghost (optional) |
| | Placebo (Vespers of the Office of the Dead, omitted before a feast of nine lessons) |
| | Compline of the Holy Ghost (optional) |
| 5:00 | COMPLINE OF OUR LADY |
| 7:00 | Bedtime prayers and devotions[2] |

We can only speculate, on the basis of monastic practice, how long these prayers took and how much time she could give to other duties. Upon awakening she would cross herself and say, "In the name of the Father ..." Kneeling on the bed with upraised arms she would recite prayers to the Holy Spirit. After dressing, she would sprinkle herself with holy water and kneel while meditating on Christ's blood. After another prayer she would kneel before the crucifix, praying to the cross and the wounds, and then before the image of the Virgin, saying five Aves. She is then ready for the office, which begins, "O Lord, open my lips, that my mouth may declare your praise."[3]

All of these devotions must have taken at least five hours a day and sometimes more. "The remaining time was available for meals, one or two a day, depending on the season, reading her rule and other books, listening to the priest's hours, giving instruction to her maid-servant, sewing on church vestments or garments for the poor, and the like."[4]

Above all, the traditional rules prescribed an attitude of penance, and sometimes harsh penitential acts, such as self-flogging. As will be shown in the discussion of penance, Julian had a mentality different from that which approved such practices. However, she followed that part of anchoritic tradition which recommended meditation on Christian charity. She may have also followed the recommendation to serve the poor through helping with their clothing, since clothing is important to her imagery.

In any case Julian focused on what is proper to all Christians, not just to anchoresses or monastics. The basic pattern of her life is intended to help all. Though in the first, short treatise she speaks at times to contemplatives as those with a special path to God, in the second version she emphasizes that what was revealed is for all her even-Christians. She claims no special privileges for herself, nor for any church group—anchoresses, nuns, or contemplatives. In this she is radically different from the ecclesiastical culture of her time, which put stress on higher and lower degrees of status among Christians, with privileges and duties matching each degree.

Even Walter Hilton, the fair-minded apostle of the "mixed life" in the fourteenth century, felt the need to enunciate the doctrine of distinction and degrees according to states of life. To comfort anchorites and all those "who enter any religious order approved in holy church" he writes:

> ... all those who are to be saved by the mercy of our
> Lord shall have a special reward and a singular honour
> in the bliss of heaven *for their state of life*, before other

souls who did not have that state in holy church,
*however holy they may be.*[5]

## *Why She Modified Her Way of Life*

It is true, of course, that St. Francis of Assisi (1182–1226)
had departed from monastic patterns. He considered secular
affairs as the proper setting for the imitation of Christ and
bore witness in the market place to his love for the neighbour.
But his innovations did not affect the role of the enclosed
nuns or solitaries, whose lives were strictly regulated and
who were warned against the evils of the secular world. Before
St. Francis, St. Benedict in the sixth century had tried to
relate monastic life to all Christians, by proposing Benedictine
communities as patterns for the organization of society. But
this ideal was diminished in the Middle Ages when the monastic movement was assimilated into feudal society, with its
divisions of social ranks and services. The monastics' role
was that of public intercessors. Their function was seen as
one of the necessary services to society, parallel to labour,
which provided the necessities of life, and to the military,
which protected the Christian state.

Even in the present day, many see the role of enclosed
religious, especially women, as those who pray in place of
others who do not. Some of the odd forms of piety, and
especially the extreme penances, were brought in because of
this theory of vicarious purchase of salvation.

Julian does not describe her role in this way. Rather, she
assumes that others, too, should share in her passionate desire
for God, finding that desire rooted in human nature, just
waiting to be nurtured. In the renewal of contemplative
orders today there is a move towards this revised concept of

contemplative religious: their circumstances make it possible for them to enrich Christian liturgy and to teach contemplative prayer.

Julian modified her way of life so that she could offer comfort to all, removing some of the misunderstandings that make the path of the Christian life an unhappy road.

## Endnotes

1. See Linda Georgiana, *The Solitary Self: Individuality in the Ancrene Wisse* (Cambridge and London, Harvard University Press, 1981).
2. Taken from Robert Ackerman, "The Liturgical Day in *Ancrene Riwle*", *Speculum* 53 (Oct., 1978): 738–9. See also *Ancrene Riwle*. Introduction and Part I, trans. Robert Ackerman and Roger Dahood, (Binghamton, N.Y., Medieval and Renaissance Texts and Studies, 1984) 37–38.
3. Ackerman 743.
4. Ackerman 742.
5. *The Scale of Perfection*. Book I, chap. 61, trans. John P.H. Clark and Rosemary Dorward, in the Classics of Western Spirituality (New York, Paulist Press, 1991) 132. However, in this same chapter, Hilton says that the "primary reward" in heaven is bestowed according to the measure of charity, and is common to all who are to be saved. A "secondary reward" is given in virtue of one's state of life. In Book II Hilton says that there is "one gate" open to contemplatives, and indicates that both "seculars and those in religious orders" may be able to enter therein (27,132). But Hilton consciously makes comparisons based on states of life.

# II

# JULIAN RE-INTERPRETS
# THE ANCHORITIC LIFE

## JULIAN ON WOMAN

Julian's message appeals to women, and to men interested
in the feminine components of spirituality, because of her
strong self-image as a woman.

This self-image was built up against great odds. Medieval
theologians admitted that women could receive the superna-
tural virtue of wisdom, as a pure gift; but they denied that
women could be endowed with natural wisdom equally with
men. Women should keep silent, while it was fitting for men
to speak. Thomas Aquinas cites an opinion that held that
woman is naturally of less dignity than man.[1] He himself
taught that "in women there is not sufficient strength of
mind to resist concupiscence."[2] Hence, good order required
that man, in whom the discernment of reason predominates,
should govern the woman, who is less wise.[3] He further held
that because the evil in the heart flows into the eye, the
woman is able to work evil on an external object, especially
if it is easily impressionable. His proof of this assertion is
his claim that the eye of a woman in her menses is able
to infect a mirror.[4] Such remarks tended to ingrain lack of
respect for women's bodies and their role in giving birth.

Julian is remarkably free of the constraints of these medieval
stereotypes. Her self-image may be garnered from (1) some

15

direct references to herself and to other women; (2) her two dream experiences of the attack of the fiend; and (3) her teaching on the equality of Christians—her "even-Christians."

## References to Women

In the early version of the *Showings*, the scribe introduces Julian in modest, but not derogatory, terms: "Here is a vision shown by the goodness of God to a devout woman, and her name is Julian, who is a recluse at Norwich and still alive, A.D. 1413, in which vision are very many words of comfort, greatly moving for all those who desire to be Christ's lovers" (ST 1).

In her early prayer she sought to be in the company of those women who were at the foot of the cross: "with Magdalene and with the others who were Christ's lovers" (LT 2). Her mother is the only one whom she specifically identifies as being at her side during her illness. Her mention of the "holy vernacle of Rome" brings to mind the legend that a woman known under the name of Veronica gave to Jesus the veil on which the likeness of his face is said to be imprinted. In Julian's first vision she sees Mary, the mother of God, as "Greater, more worthy, and more fulfilled, than everything else which God has created. ... Above her is no created thing, except the blessed humanity of Christ" (ST 4). All of these sentiments would have been sanctioned by tradition.

## A Woman-Martyr and Julian's Dream

In Julian's youth it was the story of a woman-martyr, St. Cecilia, that inspired her to ask for three wounds. The account

16

of this woman might have come to her from any of various sources. She says she heard a man of Holy Church tell the story, stressing that Cecilia died of three wounds in the neck from a sword (ST 1). Among contemporary versions of the story was that of Jacobus de Voragine in *The Golden Legend*,[5] as well as Chaucer's Second Nun's Tale in the *Canterbury Tales*. It is a sign of Julian's maturity that she interpreted the legend allegorically, conceiving of the three wounds as symbolic in her life of the wounds of contrition, compassion, and longing with her will for God.

It may be that the horror of the story of St. Cecilia still resided in her unconscious, at the time of the visions, emerging in the dream of the attack by the fiend (LT 66). The colour of her attacker was "red, like tilestone when it is newly burned, with black spots therein like speckles, fouler than the tilestone." Now before the wounds from the sword, Cecilia was put into a boiling bath to be burned. Her enemy, the prefect Almachius, put many of the saints to death in such baths for proclaiming their faith. In the end it was the sword at her neck which silenced her.

The fiend which Julian dreamed of in the shape of a young man tried to choke her: "With his paws he held me by the throat" (LT 66). "He wanted to stop my breath and kill me but he could not" (LT 66). Cecilia, who bravely taught her oppressors with the reasoning of a philosopher, was put to death for confronting the Roman prefect. Julian was risking death if she acted as a teacher and spoke out about her showings. If as a woman in the Middle Ages she would dare to speak out in the area of theology, she might indeed be burned alive. Such was the fate of Margaret Porete, and it was a fear haunting Margery Kempe. May it not be Julian's own flesh that seems to give off a stench as if she were burning? May it not be the fire that could be lit under her own body that she fears and seems to experience as she awakens?

If she can forget her experiences and put them all down to the raving of a sick woman, she will escape the witch burners and the scoffs of those who scorn woman teachers. Why else, except for fear, should Julian be so gravely tempted to forget all that she has learned? The message had led her to rapture and bliss. But to speak of it to others was to risk death. She may have anticipated facing an ecclesiastical parliament, making discordant noises and sounding like those who say prayers mindlessly. Such was the confusing jangling she hears in her dream. Or she may simply fear being silenced, which is a kind of strangling, even if she is not led to death. The devil of her dreams disrupted the peace that flowed from her visions. It is probably this experience which leads her to say that the fiend tells us what ecclesiastical tradition had long insisted on regarding women: "... thou art a wretch, a sinner, and also untrue, for you do not keep your covenant" (LT 76).

The fiend does not act alone, but with "his company" (LT 77). The fire that she smells is finally identified: it is from the fiend "who burns continually in envy" (LT 77). Helped by this insight, Julian casts off the suggestions of the fiend (and his human partners) that she concentrate merely on keeping out of sin and focus on her unworthiness as woman. Instead, she identifies clearly the source of threats to her well-being: it is raging envy. In an age which valued highly the experience of visions as signs of divine favour, she most likely did suffer from intense envy from others—even as a pastoral counsellor.

### The Teaching on Her Even-Christians

Words from one of her fellow Christians, the priest at her bedside, helped her to retain belief in her showings. When she claimed that she had raved all day, he did not blindly accept the stereotype of woman as hysterical visionary. His seriousness enabled her to reconsider. Earlier, she had been none too eager to follow the directions of the other priest at her bedside who had urged her to look at the cross: "It seemed to me that I was well as I was, for my eyes were set upwards towards heaven ... but nevertheless I agreed to fix my eyes on the crucifix...." (ST 2). She listens to the advice of others but not uncritically. Crucial to this attitude is her teaching, set forth during the first showing, that life consists in unity of love with one's even-Christians, making no distinctions between men and women.

Standing firm against the tradition that taught that women were deficient in reason, Julian takes reason as one of the three channels of her knowledge of the meaning of the showings (ST 7; LT 9). She uses here the same modes of knowing as had male theologians before her—sense, visions, reason, and spiritual insight.

She departs farthest from tradition when she ventures to speak in the name of all her even-Christians. Yet, in deference to the pressures of her time, she makes no claim initially to being a teacher: "But God forbid that you should say or assume that I am a teacher, for that is not and never was my intention; for I am a woman, ignorant, weak and frail" (ST 6). This self-deprecation is dropped totally, however, in the later text, where she speaks to all, without apology, without reference to her female sex.

She excises also from the long text her explanation that she has been taught by God, the sovereign teacher, which would seem to entitle her to instruct others. She assumes anonymity—not uncommon in the Middle Ages for both women and men—and stresses that every person's teacher is Jesus. She may be mounting an indirect defence of her right to teach in this allusion to Scripture, which says: "As for you, do not be called 'Rabbi'. You have but one teacher, and you are all brothers" (Matt. 23:8–10).

This text did not much trouble men, who taught without apology. But in the case of women, the Middle Ages held consistently to what is said in 1 Corinthians 14:35: "... if they [women] want to learn anything, they should ask their husbands at home." However, in the Scriptures some women taught and did not ask their husbands—or did not have a husband. The Fathers of the Church, nonetheless, found ways to interpret such texts in a way that seemed to justify the ban on women teachers. St. Augustine, for example, tried to reconcile the seeming disparity among the texts by affirming that women could learn directly from Jesus when he was present in his lifetime—but he did not extend this interpretation to such a claim as Julian makes: that women can teach when enlightened by Jesus in his glorified state.

We find an instance of Augustine's mind on this matter in his explication of the story of the Samaritan woman, who, after an encounter with Jesus, hastened off to teach her own people.[6] Augustine brings in the Pauline text: "But I want you to know that Christ is the head of every man, and a husband the head of his wife" (1 Cor. 11:3). Along with this he uses the familiar allegory, built on a real conception of the weakness of reason in woman, that the female stands for the senses and the male for reason; and inasmuch as reason should rule the senses, so the husband should govern the woman. Augustine also takes the occasion to digress into other biblical texts restricting the role of women, especially the rule drawn from 1 Corinthians, forbidding women to speak in the Christian assembly:

At length, wishing her to understand, Jesus saith unto her, 'Woman, call thy husband, and come thither." What means this, "Call thy husband"? Perhaps it was as the apostle says concerning women, "If they wish to learn anything, let them ask their husbands at home." But this the apostle says of that where there is no Jesus present to teach. It was said, in short, to women whom the apostle was forbidding to speak in Church. (1 Cor. 14,34)[7]

Augustine admits that the Samaritan woman is not the only one in Scripture who learned without the mediation of her husband. "Was it through her husband that He spoke to Mary, while sitting at His feet and receiving His word...?"[8] And he explains: "When the Lord Himself was at hand, and in person speaking to her, what need was there that He should speak to her by her husband?"[9]

Thus Augustine takes the position that what Jesus allowed for women when he was on earth is abrogated after the coming of the Spirit. By the use of allegory he reinforces the stereotype that woman is deficient in reason. He explains that "husband means one's understanding: as the woman should be ruled by her husband, so the soul should be ruled by reason." But this woman, the Scripture says, "has five husbands ..." (paramours)—that is, she is governed by her five unruly senses. Finally the woman "called her husband" (understanding). He "is made the head of the woman, and Christ is made the head of the man."[10] However the allegory shifts in meaning, it always presumes the weakness of woman—her carnality, her lack of understanding, and her inability to rule her own concupiscence.

Against such a tradition Julian follows through with the teacher–disciple relationship in her dialogues—with the glorified Christ, still here on earth, leading us (LT 81). Julian, of course, was in a long line of mystics and visionaries who undertook to teach others. And there had also been a few instances of male–female mutuality in monastic life.

In that context we should view Julian's special affection for St. John Beverly. When she observed his feast day, 7 May, she would also be observing the vigil of her wondrous showings, which occurred on 8 May. St. John spent part of his life as a monk in the double monastery at Whitby, while the great Abbess Hilda was in office. There he had the experience of men and women working and praying on an equal plane, with a woman presiding over both groups. Julian would have thought of him as a beloved brother religious, educated in the equality of the sexes.

Through her devotion to St. John Beverly Julian is in line with the Abbess Hilda's spirituality. The Venerable Bede, who was ordained as priest by John, writes of Hilda:

> Those under her direction were required to make a thorough study of the Scriptures and occupy themselves in good works, to such good effect that many were found fitted for Holy Orders and the service of God's altar.[11]

John was one of five men from Hilda's monastery who later became bishops.

Julian's giving advice, counselling, and comforting words to those who sought her out is also a mirror of Hilda's:

> So great was her prudence that not only ordinary folk, but kings and princes used to come to her and ask her advice in their difficulties and take it.[12] "She ... taught the observance of righteousness ... and other virtues, but especially of peace and charity."[13]

Hilda and the Anglo-Saxon nuns were not the only ones

who exemplified a state of comparative dignity for the woman. Texts in the New Testament are now being cited—especially by feminist theologians—as evidence of the calling of women to an equal status with men, "liberated from the structures of the patriarchal family and state":

> Gal. 3:28 states that baptism into the new community in Christ overcomes the social divisions of Jew and Greek, male and female, free and slave. The giving of the Spirit at Pentecost, which is the foundation of the Church, is interpreted through the prophecy of Joel about the restoration of prophetic speech in the last days of redemption. Your sons and daughters shall prophesy; prophetic speech is given to the men servants and to the maid servants. This suggests, not just an inclusion of women as Christian prophetic teachers, but a subversion of the whole hierarchical social order.[14]

If this ideal was ever actualized, it was only for a short time. Nonetheless:

> The egalitarian, prophetic concept of Church did not vanish, but it was repressed and became a counter-culture that was continually rediscovered in the Medieval and Reformation periods....[15]

This is the context in which Julian's teaching about her even-Christians should be viewed. The phrase is strongly revolutionary. It does not mean, as has been claimed by some, merely the non-clerical class. Julian makes it clear that her even-Christians are all who will be saved.

Julian's sense of herself as woman—and as on the same plane as men among her even-Christians—is supported by her metaphors of motherhood used for God and Jesus. As we shall see later, even the Lord and the Servant parable so develops as to erase inequalities.

Margery Kempe, who was threatened and persecuted for daring to speak publicly, found a sympathetic friend in Julian. Margery reports that she was inspired to seek from Julian advice about taking a vow of chastity, because "the anchoress was an expert in such things and could give good counsel." Julian recommended to Margery that she should "carry out with all her powers whatever God puts into her soul, if it were not contrary to his glory and to the profit of her fellow Christians" because "the Holy Spirit never inspires anything contrary to love." The two women, according to Margery, held holy conversation for an extended time.[16]

Julian's counsel shows respect for Margery and delicacy in dealing with the intimate converse between the soul and God. While others were applying ecclesiastical and social rules to Margery—telling her to restrain her tears, stop her preaching, change her way of dressing—Julian simply identifies the norm by which Margery can judge her own conduct. She makes her a friend and trusts her. The evidence in this encounter is enough for us to think of Julian as standing against the degrading type-casting imposed on medieval women.

## A Portrait of Julian: Summary

For all of her humility and surface self-effacement, Julian speaks with a strong, assured tone. Had she accepted the role of the submissive, inferior woman, she would have aroused no controversy. But given her strength and Gospel-based stance on the equality of all Christians, it is likely that she underwent special scrutiny and even sharp criticism. Her dream of the attacking fiend and her reluctance to speak of her showings supports this conjecture. Nonetheless, she retains faith in herself and her mission. She is a strong woman and a friend of women.

## *Endnotes*

1. *Summa Theologica* I, ques. 92, art. 1, obj. 1.
2. *Summa Theologica* II.II, ques. 149, art. 4, corpus.
3. *Summa Theologica*, I, ques. 92, art. 1, reply obj. 2.
4. *Summa Contra Gentiles*, chapter 103.
5. *Chaucer. Sources and Backgrounds*, ed. Robert P. Miller (New York, Oxford University Press, 1977) 112–120.
6. Augustine, "On the Gospel of John," Tractate 15 (Chap. 4.1–42), in *Nicene and Ante-Nicene Fathers* (New York, Charles Scribner's Sons, 1908) 7:99–107.
7. "On the Gospel of John" 103.
8. "On the Gospel of John" 103.
9. "On the Gospel of John" 103.
10. "On the Gospel of John" 105–6.
11. Venerable Bede, *A History of the English Church and People*, trans. Leo Sherley-Price. Penguin Classics (Baltimore, Md., Penguin Books, 1968) 247.
12. Bede 247.
13. Bede 247.
14. Rosemary Radford Ruether, "The Ecclesia of Patriarchy and Women Church," in *Miriam's Song II. Patriarchy: A Feminist Critique* (West Hyattsville, Md., Center for Concern, 1988) 4.
15. Ruether 4.
16. *The Book of Margery Kempe*. ed. Sanford B. Meech and Hope Emily Allen (EETS OS 212, 1940) 38.

# JULIAN AT PRAYER

From the beginning to the end of the *Showings* Julian is at prayer. Yet that does not preclude our separating out those words and attitudes which teach about prayer and which reveal the forms implicit in her practice of prayer.


## What Has Been Said

What is often said on this subject is restricted somewhat by the theories taught in both handbooks and treatises on the mystical life. We tend to look for the classical categories of prayer as thanking, petitioning, seeking pardon, and adoring. Or we search for signs of prayer as mystical union or preparation for it.

Grace Warrack in her introduction to her 1901 translation of the Long Text did not fail to note that Julian does not classify prayer according to "stages":

> Nothing is said by Julian as to successive stages of Prayer, though she speaks of different *kinds* of prayer as the natural action of the soul under different experiences or in different states of feeling or "dryness." Prayer is *asking* ("beseeching"), with submission and acquiescence; or *beholding* with the *self* forgotten, yet offered-up; it is a thanking and a praising in the heart that sometimes breaks forth into voice; or a silent joy in the sight of God as all-sufficient. And in all these ways "Prayer oneth the soul to God."[1]

These are wise words. But Julian, as we shall see, does not readily "acquiesce" when what she asks for is not given. And there are also occasions when the self is not completely forgotten in the prayer of beholding.

Father Paolo Molinari concentrates on the prayer of union in Julian.[2] E. I. Watkin presents her prayer as "practical" and as a growth in participating in God's will to become manifest in redeemed humanity:

> And it is increasingly a direct grasp by the centre of
> the soul of that Centre where all the lines of our partial
> desires and petitions converge: the Centre of the world
> process which is Its revelation.[3]

In the Introduction to the critical edition of the *Showings*, Colledge and Walsh take the position that in the Short Text Julian deals with all kinds of prayer, including vocal prayer and petitions for the well-being of the neighbour, but that in the Long Text she takes an entirely different viewpoint.[4] This is too sharp a division, given the scope of the Long Text. Maisonneuve's analysis corrects such a viewpoint, stressing that Julian's prayer is always an effort to see God beyond appearance.[5] Pelphrey's commentary expands on this view, maintaining that the "beholding" of her contemplative prayer is often only the gaze of faith—"meek, continual beholding"—and not vision at all, or at least only on occasions, with dryness following on periods of consolation. Pelphrey divides Julian's experience of prayer into petition, contemplation, and praise.[6]

These analyses are far from exhausting what is implied and stated in the *Showings* about prayer. Besides, there are some differences of opinion among the commentators. Some of these differences stem from lack of agreement on the wording and meaning of Julian's formal definition of prayer in chapter 42.

Here, then, it is useful to look at the text again, mindful of the background of the prayer tradition to which Julian was heir, yet not expecting her to mirror any particular practice or pattern.

Neither does she fit easily into any categories. But for the sake of order it can be shown that her practice includes prayers of blessing, of beholding, and of beseeching. Secondly, the wording of her treatment of prayer is obscure in some points and will be re-examined. And thirdly, for the full scope of what she intends to teach us, we need to synthesize the sections where she speaks formally of prayer.

## How Does Julian Actually Pray?

"*Blessed be God!*": The framework of all the *Showings* is the prayer, "Bless the Lord," with variations. This may be called the prayer of blessing, or of proclamation—a kind of shouting prayer. It needs to be voiced and repeated, and it is suitable for many situations. Without being a ritual, it lends itself to prayer with others. It seems to call for shouting, repeating, singing, even dancing, but always demands attentiveness to God. This attentiveness is sometimes aided by gazing on an icon or other representation, as Julian finds in keeping her eyes fixed on the crucifix. The practice differs from the one-syllable exclamation recommended by the author of the *Cloud of Unknowing*. For that writer the one-word ejaculation had for its purpose to rid the mind of all thoughts, even holy ones—yes, even the memory of the humanity of Christ—and to focus the desire on the deity. For Julian "Bless the Lord" is a short, habitual prayer, somewhat like a mantra, that rises easily to her lips. It does not become mechanical, because she adopted it in the midst of deep converse with God and uses it in moments of such encounter. It is at times an overflow of the mind into the body through excess of feeling.[7] It is an expression sometimes of praise, sometimes of thanks, sometimes of submission.

Julian utters this prayer—the first she reveals to us after

28

the petitions of her youth—"with a mighty voice". What initially causes her to break out with "Benedicite Domine"[8] is the overwhelming realization that "where Jesus is, there the Blessed Trinity is to be understood" (LT 4). Not only that, but she is deeply touched by the insight that God who is to be reverenced and feared is with us as a friend and familiar, "so homely," as she says. In the ninth showing she addresses her familiar prayer directly to Christ. She has just realized in the depth of her being that the fullness of bliss comes to us from Christ's passion. Then Christ asks: "Are you satisfied with what I have suffered for you?" And she answers: "Yes, yes, thank you, thank you; yes, indeed, Lord, blessed may you be!" (LT 22).

Also her heart bursts out with this same language of blessing when she considers that Jesus is our mother, bearing us—not to pain and death—but, in love, to joy and endless living: "Blessed may he be" (LT 60). She repeats this theme almost at once: "Our heavenly mother Jesus will not permit those of us who are his children to perish, for he is almighty, all wisdom, all love. Blessed may he be" (LT 61).

In the section where she explicitly discusses prayer at length, Julian explains this habitual outcry a little more. Rooted in part in giving thanks, the prayer also involves joyful accord with God's working, and awareness of God's mercy. It starts with inward stirrings and, growing beyond what can be held in the heart, it takes shape in words:

> And thanking also belongs to prayers. Thanking is a
> new and inner knowledge, marked by reverence and
> restrained dread, by which—enjoying and thanking
> inwardly—we attend with all our strength to the
> working that our good Lord moves us to. And
> sometimes, for its very plenitude, it breaks through into

voice, so that we say: "Good Lord, grant mercy. Blessed
may you be" (LT 41).

The passage describes how prayer becomes voiced when the
heart feels and experiences God's touch. Thus, Julian is in
the tradition of those who interpreted thanking as an offering
by the mind to God, even to the point of ineffable ecstasy,
rather than in "giving thanks" for benefits received.[9]

But if the soul is dry and without feeling, or tempted, prayer
begins in spoken words:

> ... then it is driven by reason and by grace to cry upon
> our Lord with the voice, rehearsing his blessed passion
> and his great goodness (LT 41).

The sequence is then reversed, and the spoken prayer brings
peace to the heart:

> And the power of our Lord's word turns into the soul
> and enlivens the heart and brings it by grace into
> faithful working, and makes it pray blissfully, and
> rejoice in the Lord truly (LT 41).

This instruction is confirmed by Julian's own example
when she describes her temptation and the attacks of the
fiend after the first series of showings. She was as sterile and
dry "as if she had never had any comfort." She cannot pray
inwardly. Even worse, she hears a disturbing mockery of
the practice of spoken prayer. Nonetheless, she prays
outwardly as well as she can:

> Our Lord God gave me the grace greatly to trust in
> him and to comfort my soul with bodily speech as I
> would have done for another person who was sorely
> tried ... I set my eyes on that same cross where I had
> had comfort before, reciting out loud the story of the

passion of Christ and rehearsing the beliefs of holy
Church (LT 69).

And again she uses her customary prayer, "Blessed be God",
which serves her at this time to incite devotion when it seems
to be flagging:[10]

A little smoke came in the door with a great heat and
a foul stink. And I said "Bless the Lord. Everything
in here is on fire." I thought it was a real fire that would
burn us all to death (LT 66).

She repeats her short prayer, when she learns that the fire
is an illusion of the fiend:

I asked those who were with me if they smelled any
stink. They said no, they smelled nothing. I said
"Blessed be God," for then I knew that it was the fiend
who came to disturb me (LT 66).

She takes comfort in the memory of her visions and in the
faith of the church, which are the same. This easing of her
doubts about the showings, which she must believe in without
any further external signs, occasions another prayerful proclaiming in the same words:

... he left me with his blessed word, in true
understanding, bidding me emphatically that I should
believe it. And so I do, blessed may he be (LT 70).

Lastly, Julian's prayer stands for what the people of God
will proclaim in heaven, when the new Jerusalem is realized.
It is the prayer that expresses rejoicing in the knowledge
that, indeed, all is well. What has seemed evil has been converted into a good beyond what would have otherwise have
been. Since it is in continuity with the spoken prayers on

earth, it will be some kind of proclamation fitting for risen and transformed humanity—not for separated spirits. It will become a form of "common prayer," succeeding the voiced prayers of ritual and liturgy used by the faithful on earth:

> Then none of us shall be inclined to say in any way:
> "Lord, if things had been thus and so, then all would
> have been well." But we shall all say with one voice,
> "Lord, blessed may you be. For things are thus, and
> all is well" (LT 85).

What has served Julian as an external expression of prayer, both in time of comfort and of woe, now links to the eternal beatitude which she has longed for. This double use of her spoken prayer will help in determining what she intended when she formally defined prayer.

But first it may not be fully clear why this prayer could be so all-embracing and central to Julian, and potentially to us, to whom she seems to recommend it. The wording is not common in our everyday speech, but this prayer of proclamation is still used in devotional and liturgical rituals. It is deeply embedded in tradition and Scripture.

In many of the psalms the prayer of proclamation takes the form of blessing the Lord. For example, Psalm 104 uses a blessing to celebrate the glories of creation:

> Bless the LORD, O my soul!
> O LORD, my God, you are great indeed!
> You are clothed with majesty and glory,
>     robed in light as with a cloak (Ps. 104:1–2).

Frequent in liturgical use is the canticle of the three young men in the fiery furnace (Dan. 3:52–90). But given the variations in the usages of the blessing, it is helpful to return to Julian's text to find the sense in which she uses "blessed," and hence what she means when she proclaims a blessing.

The nearest she comes to defining the degrees (that is, the categories) of bliss[11]—and hence the sense in which she uses the word—occurs in the sixth showing (LT 14). There she says that the bliss which the "blessed" will experience means that (1) God will honour and give recognition to each of them; (2) this honour and recognition will be made known to all others, together with the service each one has done; and (3) this honour bestowed in such a personal way will be forever, and forever fresh and new. Here, too, for Julian one's even-Christians are part of the beatitude of eternal life.

That God is our reward in such a complete way gives sufficient meaning to bliss and blessed when applied to humanity. But Julian blesses God, and calls God and divine works blessed, many times and with many variations, so that the word is made to bear multiple meanings.

There are some expected uses. "Blessed" precedes her naming and addressing the Trinity; the Godhead; Christ, and his humanity, face, kindness, body, blood, head, will, breast; presence; heavenly clothing; soul; dying; word; behests. She calls Christ the blessed Saviour and the king of bliss. His mother is our blessed lady, and the members of his body are blessed creatures. Also the passion is blissful, in the sense of bringing us to joy and bliss. In this context sin will be no shame, but will be an occasion for increased bliss, with the sinner being "blissfully restored" without end (LT 38)

*Prayer of Beholding*: Hinging on this prayer, which takes so many forms, is another prayer—that of beholding. In our effort to fit Julian into traditional practices of prayer, we are inclined to see this prayer as passive, in contrast to the activity which is manifestly part of prayer that can be uttered.

33

But for Julian this is not always so. Perhaps it is never so. For in prayer the opposite of activity may be spontaneity rather than passivity.

In any case, Julian describes beholding as an activity with many forms. Not all of the beholdings preclude concern for our own needs or puzzlement over the human condition. Beholding, which is more than seeing, may contain thought, an angle of judgment, even feelings and emotions. It is not a pure act of will though it is often regulated by choice. True, there is a form of beholding which is pure gift (LT 41), but it is not the only kind. In general, it consists in fixing the heart on God, with a concomitant overflow into the understanding.

The effects of the prayer of beholding are explained in the first showing: "... the beholding and loving of the maker makes the soul seem least in its own sight, most fills it with reverent dread and true meekness, and with abundance of charity for one's even-Christians" (LT 6). These effects are exemplified in Mary:

And to teach us this ... our Lord God showed our lady
St. Mary ... the beholding of God filled her with
reverent dread ... and with meekness. And on this
foundation she was made full of grace and of all manner
of virtues ... (LT 7)

Julian's own prayer of beholding in the first showing takes in all that God has made, and she attends to what she sees diligently. She recommends this prayer to all, trusting that they will be taught truly thereby and find comfort. The lesson is that to love our even-Christians rightly is to love God and all that is (LT 9). Rejecting the limited human way of presuming to separate what is good from what is evil, the one who prays thus turns to the beholding of God and all divine works (LT 11).

But Julian herself is not always able to do this, because of sin and evil. In the thirteenth showing, for example, she laments the human condition:

> In this I stood beholding generally—in sorrow and mourning—saying then to our Lord in my intention with very great dread: "Ah, good Lord, how can all be well considering the great damage that has come to creatures through sin?" And here I desired to have a clearer explanation wherewith I might be put at ease (LT 29).

Another aspect of beholding is an awareness of how God beholds us, loving us without imputing blame for our sin (LT 49). We can focus our beholding on the truth that the restoring of humanity was greater than the harm done by sin (LT 29). And though we sin, God beholds us continually and with eternal foresight (LT 85).

Scattered throughout are some bits of instructions on the prayer of beholding. The source of beholding is wisdom, and from beholding, when joined to truth, which sees God, issues love and delight in God (LT 44). Julian's own experience of beholding in the visions is complex, joining the feeling of love and security coming from the showings with a background consciousness of the teachings of faith. The accord between these two assures her that the showings were from God (LT 46). Another form of complex beholding involves giving attention to the fact that we will sin, though we must not concentrate on the beholding of the self:

> ... the higher beholding keeps us in spiritual comfort and true enjoyment in God; ... the lower beholding

35

keeps us in dread and makes us ashamed of ourselves.
But our good Lord wants us to give more attention to
the beholding of the higher than of the lower, until
the time that we are brought up above, where we have
Jesus as our reward ... (LT 82).

Julian tells us more and more about this prayer. She beholds
the Trinity in Jesus, and likewise God's motherhood (LT
55). "The fullness of joy is to behold God in all" (LT 35).
The highest joy is to behold the great deed to be done at
the end of time, by God working through humanity, making
all things well (LT 36). We are not, however, to try to
behold exactly what that deed shall be (LT 33). Rather, in
a spirit of thanks, we are to pray for the deed to be done
(LT 42).

Of the higher beholding she says again: "to be wholly given
to the beholding of him is a higher prayer, which cannot
be perceived" (LT 43).

In fact, all lesser forms of beholding are really seeking—and
seeking serves us just as well. The pinnacle of beholding,
worked in us by special grace, adds the dimension of delight:
"When we, of his special grace, plainly behold him, feeling
no other needs, then we follow him and he draws us to him
in love" (LT 43). Again, such a prayer should not be described
as "passive", but as spontaneous, under the strong impulse
of grace. This experience is a "high, powerful desire to be
made one" with God, "centred in his dwelling" (or entering
into it), and delighting in his goodness.[12]

By such a special grace Julian beholds the joy that is to
come:

And then our Lord opened my spiritual eye and showed
me my soul in the midst of my heart. I saw the soul

as large as if it were a blissful kingdom. And by the conditions that I saw therein I understood that it is a splendid city. In the midst of that city sits our Lord Jesus, God and man ... Jesus will never withdraw from the place that he takes in the soul, for in us is his home where he is most at home, and his dwelling where he abides forever (LT 67).

And just as the blessing prayer finds its completeness in heaven, so the prayer of beholding lasts forever: "The creature shall see and endlessly behold God" (LT 43).

*The Beseeching Prayer:* The third form of prayer is the one with which we are most familiar—the prayer of beseeching. Julian does not discourage us from asking for what we need. In fact, we are moved by grace to petition for what God intends to give us. Beseeching also has a range of purposes—from the simple asking for our basic needs to the prayer for the presence of God. Unlike many other teachers of prayer, she does not draw a sharp line between earthly things and those of heaven.[13] Rather, God wishes us to ask for all that he has decided to do (LT 42). We must simply pray aright—that is, for what is good for us—and steadfastly trust (LT 41). Beseeching is natural to us because the "kind yearning" of our soul is to have God, and it is God's yearning to have us.

If we tire of asking because our beseeching does not seem to be answered, we are to wait yet longer, or await more grace, or a better gift (LT 42). It was, for example, "a better gift" that came to Julian after she prayed without receiving a bodily vision of Mary. Beseeching is the prayer that enables us to pray always, for it is "a true, gracious, enduring will of the soul, united and fastened to the will of our Lord, by the sweet, mysterious working of the Holy Ghost" (LT 41).

## Uncertainties in the Text

Against this background of the actual practice of prayer it should now be possible to understand a little more completely Julian's definition of prayer (LT 42).

There are two competing versions of that definition. Both versions agree on the opening line: "For prayer is a right understanding of that fullness of joy that is to come, with intense longing and steadfast trust." On the next lines there is disagreement. The editors of the critical edition, following their reading of the Paris manuscript, say: "The savouring or seeing of our bliss, to which we are ordained, by nature makes us to long; true understanding and love, with a sweet recollection in our savour, by grace makes us to trust." Those who follow the Sloane manuscripts say, rather: "Failing of our bliss that we are by nature ordered to, makes us to long. True understanding and love, with a sweet recollection of our Saviour, by grace makes us to trust."[14] The difference matters considerably for understanding Julian. The evidence from the whole text lends authority to the Sloane reading. While the other definition rests on an experience of mystical union—"savouring or seeing our bliss" and the recollection of this "savour"—the preferred version does not. It offers a definition which can cover the whole range of prayer—in faith, in vision, in dryness, in joy, in blessing, beholding, and beseeching. As we have seen above Julian presents all prayer as rooted in the whole of life, in time and in eternity, and does not differentiate between any "true" prayer and the higher manifestations of it. This position is also in harmony with Julian's stance towards her audience—her even-Christians, all the people of God, not all of whom have the gift of the higher forms of mystical prayer.

Hence, it is probable that Julian defines prayer thus, dividing its "workings"—its active components—into longing and trust:

> For prayer is a right understanding of that fullness of joy that is to come, with intense longing and steadfast trust. Falling short of that bliss which we are by nature ordered to, causes us to long; true understanding and love—with a sweet awareness of our Saviour—by grace makes us to trust. And in these two workings our Lord beholds us always (LT 42).

This definition is in accord with Julian on many points:

> The Sloane version of Julian's definition ... does not exclude mystical prayer, though it is not limited to it. Indeed, the Sloane form implies the full continuum of the work of the Trinity, in whom "kynde"[15] is rooted, with whom "kynde" is bonded, and by whom "kynde" is indwelt. The latter part of the definition, especially, implies those graces which feed and nurture "kynde" until it blossoms into Christlikeness.[16]

Julian's words should enlighten all who pray:

> The definition therefore includes all special sights, savorings, and touchings, even such as enabled Julian to speak in the language of the senses about Christ glorified, whom she beheld in the twelfth revelation. But the Sloane form can also—and this is essential, given Julian's intended audience—include that prayer which springs from common graces and augments trust, when a troubled and tempested mind dwells gently on the Savior in loving faith.[17]

In fact, the definition even supports the assurance Julian gives that all our living is prayer in God's sight, for God accepts our good will, however we may feel (LT 41).

Another contested passage should be reviewed here. It is Christ's exhortation to Julian to pray under all circumstances:

> Pray inderly though you think it brings no savour, for it is profitable though you feel nothing, though you see nothing. Yes, pray though you think that you cannot. For in dryness and barrenness, in meekness and in feebleness—in such a time your prayer is very pleasing to me, though you think you have no relish for it (LT 41).

The crucial word is *inderly* (or *interly*). It has been variously translated "interiorly" or "wholeheartedly." Neither choice seems adequate nor fully consistent with the context. "Interiorly" cannot be meant, for in this same chapter Julian tells us how she herself prays "when the heart is dry and feels nothing." She is propelled "by reason and grace" to pray out loud, reciting the narrative of the passion and speaking of the goodness of God. "Wholeheartedly" does not satisfy, since the soul cannot muster any enthusiasm for the effort in a state of dryness. The word seems to mean "from the heart" in the sense of sincerely, free of the mechanical use of words, real rather than in appearance only.[18] Those who recite prayers mechanically thus fail to pray "inderly".

A less significant difference, as it relates to the actual practice of prayer, is the wording which describes the voice of the blessed in heaven. The Sloane text, as we noted above, refers to that eternal chorus as "without voice". The Paris text says, "with one voice" (LT 85). It is possible that Julian intends to draw on the liturgy of the Roman mass, wherein exalted words of praise are like those of the angelic seraphim. The scriptural source reads: "'Holy, holy, holy is the Lord of hosts!' they, the seraphim, cried one to the other. 'All the earth is filled with his glory!'" (Is. 6:3).[19] "Without voice" as in the Sloane text has the advantage of suggesting the new state in which risen humanity will live, a state in which the sounds and sights of earthly usage will be perceived differently. For if the prayer of ecstatic beholding is "unperceivable" and beyond voice here, so much the more beyond perception will be that utterance which comes from the "blissful beholding" of the saints in heaven.

## A Synthesis of Her Teaching

With these uncertainties interpreted, it now remains to look briefly at the scope and focus of Julian's central instruction on prayer. In the first showing she incorporates a section stressing that the centre of our prayer is the goodness of God. Hence, means or mediators are to be included only if we see in them a sign of God's goodness. In fact, we may use these "many means" out of ignorance and misunderstanding. Not even Mary, his mother, is needed as a means for diverting divine anger from us, for there is no such anger. Rather, we join with the holy ones of heaven as dear friends, approaching a good God familiarly (LT 6).

What prayers does she recommend? First, blessing: a spontaneous response to God's goodness. Second, beholding: with his grace and help we are to stand "in spiritual beholding" marvelling at the love God has for us "of his goodness." Third, beseeching: since our whole yearning is to have God, we may ask of God whatever we desire in our "kindly will"— our natural inclining to the good. It will be "right" and good for us. Such prayer fills us with love for our even-Christians, too.

In later chapters (41–43) in the fourteenth showing she finds a need to deal with the difficulties in "beseeching"—with the problem of what we should pray for and how we should cope with our dryness and lack of trust. The answer to the first comes as a sudden insight: God, dwelling within us, moves us to ask for what is right; and so loving us, wills that we have it. That is what beseeching is—a movement rooted in the oneness of the human with the divine will, and stirred to action by the Holy Spirit. And when the soul lets itself realize what God is doing and has done, it breaks forth in blessing. The fruit of such prayer is to make us more like the one to whom we address ourselves.

Our unlikeness is in the sinful condition of humanity. At this point in her reflections Julian has looked at the horror of sin and also at the great deed that will make all things well. We are to pray because it is the will of God to make us "partners" in the deed that is being done (LT 43). Thus, the goodness which Julian attended to at the beginning now appears as the fulfilment of all our powers, all our human capabilities and longings (LT 43). All of this is a new stimulus to beholding, whether in dryness or in comfort. The beholding extends to realizing how God's goodness is at work in everything. The eternal beholding enables us both to truly know ourselves and to have God in fullness.

Thus Julian teaches us blessing, beholding, and beseeching in the full scope of our lives.

She teaches prayer as "oneing" with God. It is a practical way of union with God, for which she had petitioned.

### Endnotes

1. Grace Warrack, ed. *Revelations of Divine Love. Recorded by Julian of Norwich Anno Domini 1373* (London, Methuen Co., 1901), introduction, xxxix.

2. Paolo Molinari, S.J., *Julian of Norwich. The Teaching of a 14th Century English Mystic* (New York, Norwood Editions, 1977).

3. *On Julian of Norwich, and In Defense of Margery Kempe* (Exeter, University of Exeter, 1979) 30.

4. *A Book of Showings* I, 114–133, especially 116.

5. Roland Maisonneuve, *L'Univers Visionnaire de Julian of Norwich*. Diss. University of Paris—Sorbonne, 1978 (Paris: privately printed) I, 417.

6. *Love Was His Meaning* 214–54.

7. Thomas Aquinas offers this as one of three reasons for voiced prayer, citing the psalmist: "Therefore my heart is glad and my soul rejoices,/My body, too, abides in confidence." (Ps. 16,9). (ST II.II, ques. 83, art. 12, corpus).

8. Colledge and Walsh cite F. Cabrol, "Benedicite et Benedictus es Domine", as evidence of the differing forms the word too. But they do not include Cabrol in the bibliography. *A Book of Showings* I, 211, note 17.

9. See ST II.II, ques. 83, art. 17, corpus, where Thomas Aquinas cites, but rejects, this meaning of thanksgiving as found in St. Basil. Father John-Julian, OJN, says that *thankyng* in Julian "must be understood to be an act of the will and of the mind opening to God's own will." '*Thankyng* in Julian,"*Mystics Quarterly* 15 (June, 1989), 70–73.

10. Thomas Aquinas gives this as the first of his three reasons for vocal prayer: "in order to incite interior devotion, whereby the mind of the person praying is raised to God, because by means of external signs, whether of words or of deeds, the human mind is moved as regards apprehension, and consequently also as regards the affections." ST II.II, ques. 83, art. 12, corpus.

11. *A Book of Showings* I, 230, note 1.

12. Colledge and Walsh render this "entende to his motion." They read the Sloane mss. as "entred to his wowyng." Glasscoe transcribes the phrase as "centred to his wonying." The sense of

the text may well be, "to center oneself in God's dwelling"—in the city of the heart and the kingdom of God.

13. Thomas Aquinas teaches that prayer should be "orderly": that is, we should prefer spiritual to carnal goods, and heavenly to earthly ones. (*Collationes De Pater Noster, et Credo in Deum.*)
14. For a fuller development of this question see Ritamary Bradley, "Julian of Norwich on Prayer," *Analaecta Cartusiana* 106, ed. James Hogg (Salzburg, Institut für Anglistik und Amerikanistik, Universität Salzburg, 1983) I, 136–54.
15. "Kynde" (kind) refers to nature in this context.
16. "Julian of Norwich on Prayer" 154.
17. "Julian of Norwich on Prayer" 154.
18. The same word—*inderly*—occurs again in Chapter 66, where it is said that, upon hearing Julian say she had raved, the priest laughed aloud and "*inderly*." Colledge and Walsh, who reject "interiorly" as a translation, explain their choices in footnotes to Chapter 21 (ST) and Chapters 41 and 66 (LT). But "wholeheartedly", which they select for their translation, seems scarcely the best equivalent. *MED* defines *enterli* (adv.) as sincerely or devoutly. With verbs of asking, *enterli* can mean "earnestly or heartily," but in Julian's usage in these texts, "pray" is not specifically a word of asking.
19. Such is the interpretation of Colledge and Walsh, *A Book of Showings* II, 719, note 14.

# PENANCE AND PUNISHMENT

The official Visitor assessing Julian's way of living the anchoritic life would be expected to inquire about her fidelity to practices of penance. Her answer is embodied in the *Showings*. She was reshaping the anchoritic rule in this regard, as well as in the programme of prayer. It required courage on Julian's part to take such a stance, for tradition was against her.

But Julian would have been chiefly concerned with those among her even-Christians who came to her to find out how to integrate penitential practices into their own lives.[1] Accustomed as they were to the extreme practices of the self-mutilating flagellants, and acquainted with some instruction in the ascetical life, they found in Julian an original counsellor.

Union with God in medieval handbooks is the peak of a tripartite progression: "... starting with purgation, in which the self recognizes its unworthiness, moving to illumination, in which the mystic learns to see the true nature of things, and finally [to] union, in which the will of the mystic is united with God/Truth."[2] While Julian does indeed deal with these three components of the mystical life, she does so in a unique way and by moving back and forth among them, and without a set sequence. The structure of her way of life comes, rather, from what she had asked for in her youthful prayer—though not in the same order: contrition, compassion and intentional union with God.

Her stance on contrition, in particular, which is especially proper to the purgative way, differs sharply from that of the monastic tradition in which she had been formed. Penance and satisfaction for sin was a governing idea in that tradition. And the guilt of sin, together with human vulnerability before the attacks of fiends, dictated a sombre demeanour and restraint in manners. Laughter was, at best, thought unseemly.

## This Life is a Prison

The emphasis on penance was built into the anchoritic lifestyle. In the first place the Office for the Enclosing of Anchorites, with its rules to be observed by both sexes, stresses penance in a harsh metaphor—that of prison. The bishop—or his representative—presiding at the enclosure ceremony for the woman, instructed the applicant thus: "Let her [the anchoress] think that she is convicted of her sins and committed to solitary confinement as to a prison, and that on account of her own weakness she is unworthy of the fellowship of mankind."[3]

This metaphor finds its way into Julian's text, but its meaning is essentially changed. No harshness remains in Christ's words to her about penance. We ought first to forgive ourselves:

> ... he [Christ] says: "... I do not want you to be heavy-
> hearted or overly sorrowful. I can tell you that no
> matter how you act you will have woe. And therefore
> I want you to understand penance wisely, and you will
> then see that all your living is a profitable penance"
> (LT 77).

And it is likely that the prison to which she refers is everyone's "place", rather than the cell where the anchoress is held in solitary confinement: "This place is a prison, and this life is penance, and he wants us to have enjoyment in the remedy" (LT 77).[4]

The "remedy" is that the prison warden (the one who keeps us) is none other than Christ: "He that will be our bliss when we are there (in fullness of joy), that same one is our keeper while we are here" (LT 77). From the prison of the human condition she says—praying, as always, to God's goodness:

> I know full well that I have a vexing pain.
> But our Lord is almighty and can punish greatly;
> And he is all wisdom and can punish me for my good;
> And he is all goodness and loves me most tenderly
> (LT 77).

By expanding the prison metaphor to include her fellow Christians, and by taking away its tone of vindication, Julian draws others into her own experience. She consoles those who feel trapped in difficult situations, those who have lost control over where they go and what they do, the sick who are confined, the poor who are imprisoned by their poverty, the oppressed who are limited in their access to what they need—all, in fact, who experience the constraints of the human condition. "The Lord is with us, keeping and leading us into joyous fulfilment" (LT 77).

Though Julian had embraced a way of life in great part dedicated to voluntary penance what she says on this subject is not marked by a narrow, ascetical tone:

> The penance that man takes on himself was not shown to me—that is, it was not shown specifically. But it was shown, specifically and in an exalted way, and in a beautiful way, that we ought meekly and patiently put up with and endure the penance that God himself gives us—keeping in mind his blessed passion (LT 77).

This, her principal teaching on penance, is part of a summary section wherein she tells us the various ways in which God was revealed to her, both in heaven and on earth. The chief dwelling place of God is the human soul, "God's resting place and honourable city." God wants us to fix our attention on that dwelling place, finding in it more enjoyment in his love than sorrow over our frequent failings. Again, she says that penance is a necessary part of living:

> The greatest honour that we can give to God is to live—gladly and merrily—for his love. For he loves us so

tenderly that he sees all our living and our penance (LT 81).

The very longing of our heart for what we love"—"kind loving"—he sees in us as a continual penance. Even more— God also endures a kind of penance, in his longing for us, his permitting us to live here—"and from this viewpoint he will see our penance":

> For this is our natural penance, and the highest, as I
> see it; for this penance is always with us and will last
> until we reach fulfillment, when we shall have God as
> our reward. ... He accomplishes this penance in us, and
> mercifully helps us to bear it ... He wants us, therefore,
> to set our hearts on what is to come (LT 81).

Then the courteous Lord reiterates the lesson:

> "I know well that you desire to live for my love,
> merrily and gladly suffering all the penance that comes
> to you; and inasmuch as you do not live without sin,
> you want to suffer for my love all the woe, tribulation,
> and discomfort that might befall you ... But do not
> be greatly disturbed by the sin that befalls you against
> your will" (LT 82).

Then, in a link with the central parable of the *Showings*, she specifies the reason for this teaching: the Lord looks on the Servant with pity, and not with blame. Julian knows of no lover of Christ who is continually kept from sin, but all are kept securely in God. To behold the sinful self is a matter of truth, but it is not the highest truth, which is to behold God. In that beholding, in falling and rising "we are preciously kept in one love" (LT 82).

What that promise means, and the ground of it, is taught

in the parable of the Lord and the Servant. And only in the light of that lesson can we understand how it is that we should live in holy delight.

## We Laugh . . . Christ Does Not

Monastic rules did not advocate living merrily. In fact, it was a commonplace in those rules that monastics and serious Christians who imitated them did not laugh. Julian departs radically from these strictures and says:

> Also I saw our Lord mocking the malice of the fiend
> and bringing his might to nothing. And he wills that
> we do the same. At this sight [the powerlessness of the
> fiend] I laughed heartily—which made them laugh that
> were around me. And I thought: How I wish that all
> my even-Christians had seen as I saw. Then they would
> all have laughed with me. But I did not see Christ
> laughing: it was the sight he showed me. I well know
> it was that which made me laugh. Yet I understood that
> we may laugh in order to comfort ourselves, and to
> rejoice in God—for the fiend is overcome (LT 13).

Therapeutic laughter, we might call it today, a laughter that destroys negative thoughts and replaces them with positive ones. But the monastic prescriptions against merriment were built on the notion that the sinner should not laugh, while still in a state of pilgrimage, where he might at any time be waylaid by the devil, like a highway robber. This view was founded in part on the New Testament, which expected the just to postpone their laughter until the day of the eschaton: "Blessed are you who are now weeping,/for you will laugh" (Luke 6:21) "Woe to you who laugh now,/for you will grieve and weep" (Luke 6:25). Also, in the New Testament, the laughter of the multitude often took the form of scorn and disbelief in Christ. For example, the multitude laughs when Jesus summons a dead girl to awaken (Matt. 9:24; Mk. 5:40; Luke 8:53). From such a context, as interpreted by the Fathers and incorporated into monastic rules, monastics, hermits, and anchorites were to refrain from laughter, or at least to laugh with restraint. Seriousness of purpose and ascetic discipline for the most part precluded merriment. That was the mark of those given to the pleasures of this present world.

John Chrysostom, who rebuked even lay people for laughing, asks "how the solitary can laugh when he must mourn for this world and be crucified to the world."[5]

Furthermore, Christ, the model of monks, was said—again according to St. John Chrysostom—never to have laughed. (This claim is put in the mouth of Jorge de Burgos by Umberto Eco in the novel *The Name of the Rose*). Medieval theologians argued the point, affirming on the one hand that since Christ is fully human and laughter is a mark of humanity, Christ must have laughed. But they were countered by the argument that Christ needed only have the power of laughter, but did not have to exercise it. Why did he not laugh? Most often adduced as a reason was the character of the Man of Sorrows, who shed tears instead of showing merriment.

Also, the Christ of the New Testament revealed God in a fullness that had not been the case in the Hebrew Scriptures. In those books God is depicted as laughing in more than one situation. What bearing had this, we may wonder, on the rule against laughing? Gregory the Great has an explanation:

> When God is said to laugh at the plight of the wicked
> (Prov. 1:26), one must understand this to mean that He

is unwilling to show them mercy. This is a just and appropriate "laughter."

More difficult to explain, however, is the account of God laughing at the pains of the innocent:

> How can God, above all, display this type of seemingly inappropriate laughter? Is it not an evil to laugh at the suffering of the innocent? Here, Gregory explains, God's laugh is not out of scorn, for the only pains the innocent suffer are the pains of unsatisfied desire. What do they desire? God Himself. Therefore, God is said to laugh at the pains of the innocent, which are nothing less than their constant and unyielding desire to be united to Him. His laughter is the laughter of Abraham and not of Sarah.[6]

Hence Gregory concludes: God's laughter "is appropriate because of the attitude which precedes it, and the object which evinces it."[7]

Such were the extraordinary efforts by the Fathers of the Church to maintain the rule against monastic laughter, even in the face of scriptural texts that seemed to point to contrary norms. The Middle Ages never wholly resolved the tension, cited above, between the arguments that Christ did not laugh because of his overwhelming sorrow, and yet that he should have laughed as a sign of his full humanity.

Another theme may have influenced medieval efforts to show that the true Christ did not laugh. In some Gnostic traditions wherein it is taught that Christ is not fully human, but only took on the appearance of humanity, he is portrayed as laughing at the crucifixion since he did not really die: the figure on the cross is an illusion and has thus thwarted the efforts of the devil to confound him.[8]

It is in the setting of this grimly-fought theological and monastic context that Julian goes contrary to the rules that were in force. She laughs forthrightly and encourages us to laugh: "I understood that it is all right to laugh both in comforting ourselves and in rejoicing in God" (LT 13). Nothing in mainstream asceticism or monastic rules would have sanctioned this merriment, especially in relation to contrition for sin.

In so doing, however, she is supported by many texts in the Hebrew Scriptures. For the exiled Israelites returning to Sion, there is laughter: "Then our mouth was filled with laughter,/and our tongue with rejoicing" (Ps. 126:2). Bildad encourages Job to laugh: "Once more will he fill your mouth with laughter, and your lips with rejoicing" (Job 8:21). The innocent and the just may laugh in joy at the goodness of God and in scorn of the evil of wrongdoers. Such, too, was in the example of St. Cecilia, who laughed in scorn at the powerlessness of Almachius, the wicked prefect.

Most commentators were still reluctant to think of God as laughing, however, even in metaphor. Augustine is evidence of this in his commentary on the second Psalm: "He who is throned in heaven laughs;/the LORD derides them" (v. 4). In an ingenious turn in interpreting the text, Augustine protests:

> Nothing of this however must be taken in a carnal sort,
> as if God either laugheth with the cheek, or derideth
> with nostril; but it is to be understood of that power
> which He giveth to His saints, that they seeing things
> to come, namely that the Name and rule of Christ is
> to pervade posterity and possess all nations, should

understand that these men "meditate a vain thing"
[verse 1]. For this power whereby these things are
foreknown is God's "laughter" and "derision." "He
that dwelleth in the heavens shall laugh them to scorn."
If by these "heavens" we understand holy souls, by
these God, as foreknowing what is to come, will "laugh
them to scorn" and "have them in derision."[9]

But why does not Julian see Christ laughing? She does not
explain. She later reports that she sees Christ alternately with
a glad countenance and with a sorrowful one. In this way,
without contradicting the theologians, she suggests a balance
in our way of beholding Christ, who is so far from being
a stranger that he is always familiar and friendly.

Though she did not see Christ laughing at the evil of the
fiend, she does hear him referring to joy, even in connection
with the passion, when he beholds those for whom he suffered
and died:

Then our good Lord said, asking: "Are you well pleased
that I suffered for you?" I said: "Yea, good Lord, by
your mercy: yea, good Lord, blessed may you be."
Then said Jesus our good Lord: "If you are well pleased,
I am pleased. It is a joy, a bliss, and an endless delight
to me that ever I suffered the passion for you. And if
I could suffer more, I would suffer more" (LT 22).

Clearly, then, Julian comes down on the side of joy. And
though Christ did not laugh in the first instance when the
fiend was shown, he does in a later vision express one of
the motivations which underlies laughter—namely, scorn for
the devil who tries to thwart the divine will: "Also I saw
our Lord scorn the fiend's malice and despise his powerlessness ... we may laugh because the devil is overcome. Then

I saw him scorn his malice ... I see scorn in that God scorns
him and he shall be scorned ... And I said, "he is scorned",
meaning that God scorns him: that is to say, he sees him
now as he shall be without end, for in this God shows that
the fiend is damned" (LT 13).[10]

Only the devil is described as "punished." His punishment
is that he will see that the villainy he has done has only
served to increase the joy of his victims. And all the pain
and tribulation he has aimed at them will go into hell. They
will laugh, both in scorn and in joy.

## Satisfaction for Sin

But the aftermath of sin is still to be reckoned with. The
devotional and ascetical writings current in Julian's time presented this reckoning in harsh terms. God was thought of
as taking vengeance when evils befall us in this world, as
well as in the hellfire that awaits the sinner. The language
was often that of a legal debt exacted by a just and demanding
God. The sinner owes a debt that he is unable to pay.

St. Ambrose describes humanity, burdened with the debt
of sin, as liable to a hard creditor who could be satisfied
with nothing less than the death of the debtor. Then Jesus
came, to offer his death for the death of all.[11] From the time
of St. Anselm attention was riveted on the passion almost
solely as a work of satisfaction—giving back to an angry God
what sin had robbed him of.[12]

Julian's tone and teaching are strikingly different, though
her approach is not confrontational. We do indeed owe a
debt. We "owe" to God the faithful doing of his bidding.
This debt "is fulfilled in the true loving of God, a blessed
love which Christ accomplishes in us" (LT 60). The eyes

of the Father are not blazing in anger towards sinners, but full of pleasure at the Son's working, which he rewards with a prize. That prize is the gift of humanity, healed by the medicine of the passion:

> The working of the Father is this: he gives a prize to his Son, Jesus Christ ... the Father could not have given him a prize that would have pleased him more ... The Father is well-pleased with all the deeds that Jesus has done concerning our salvation. Wherefore we belong to him not only by his buying us, but also by the courteous gift of his Father. We are his joy, his prize, his source of honor. We are his crown (LT 22).

When Julian uses the language of debt, Christ is the debtor, who "owes" us the unqualified love of motherhood:

> He could no more die, but he would not cease from working. Wherefore it is needful for him to feed us, for the precious love of motherhood which has made him debtor to us (LT 60).

Julian indeed acknowledges that humanity could not lift itself out of the morass of sin:

> And thus our Lord wills that we accuse ourselves, intentionally and truly seeing and knowing our falling and all the harm that comes thereof; and seeing and knowing that we can never restore it (LT 52).

But Christ came for our sake, not to ward off the vengeance of the Father. Where teachers such as St. Anselm taught that Christ took on our sinful flesh to suffer the wrath of an angry God in our stead, Julian reverses the statement. She reasons that precisely because of our unity with Christ, we are always in God's love: "Our Father cannot, nor will not, assign any more blame to us than to his own Son, the beloved Christ" (LT 51).

That there is no wrath in God has long been a stumbling block for many readers, who can otherwise find themselves in agreement with Julian's teaching. Traces of this teaching appear in early ecclesiastical writers, but even then with harsh nuances not found in Julian. Augustine, for example, in commenting on Psalm 2:5, "Then He shall speak unto them in His wrath, and vex them with His sore displeasure", interprets the words so as to soften the image of a punishing God. God's "vengeance" is to remind creatures of their role as servants:

> ... by the wrath and sore displeasure of God must not
> be understood any mental perturbation; but the might
> whereby He most justly avengeth, by the subjection of
> all creatures to His service. For that is to be observed
> and remembered which is written in the Wisdom of
> Solomon, "But Thou, Lord of power, judgest with
> tranquility, and with great favour orderest us."[13]

Or this wrath can also be understood "as that darkening of the mind, which overtakes those who transgress the law of God." In any case, God's wrath is not in God, but in us:

> The "wrath" of God then is an emotion which is
> produced in the soul which knoweth the law of God,
> when it sees this same law transgressed by sinners.[14]

But in a theme that never appears in Julian Augustine seems to justify the taking of vengeance of one person on another in God's name: "For by this emotion of righteous souls many things are avenged."[15]

On the subject of contrition it is especially important to

note that Julian continues to address her even-Christians, not distinguishing between laity and persons in orders. As a member of an order in the broad sense—that of anchoresses—Julian is heir to a teaching that relates penance to a sharp difference between monk and layman and applies that difference to both sexes. The monk has an edge on making satisfaction for his sin—on restoring the right relation that sin disrupted. God was said to judge the monk more mildly than the non-professed, more mildly than anyone not living in an order—providing the monk is faithful:

> For although both [monk and layman] may commit the same sin, yet if from his whole heart the monk repents having sinned, and with fervent love keeps the rule to which he has submitted himself, he will obtain greater mercy than the layman, however much the layman who is still held back in the world repents. But if the monk should not want to repent, he will be subjected to a greater damnation than the layman.[16]

But Julian beholds God making no distinction between her state under vow and herself in her youth; nor between any person in an order and her even-Christians—all who will be saved. She keeps an attitude of contrition throughout her life and exhorts all others to do the same. Such is Julian's way.

### Endnotes

1. For a study of this subject through the tenth century see Allen J. Frantzen, *The Literature of Penance in Anglo-Saxon England* (New Brunswick, N.J., Rutgers University Press, 1983).

2. A. Leslie Harris, "The Mystic Vision in the *Optimist's Daughter*", *Studies in the Humanities* 13 (June, 1986): 32. See also Dom David Knowles, *The English Mystical Tradition* (New York, Harper, 1977) 21–38.

3. Appendix A., "The Office for the Enclosing of Anchorites (according to the use of Sarum)", in Rotha Clay, *Hermits and Anchorites of England* (London, Methuen and Co., 1914) 193. Similar petitions occurred in other forms of Enclosure ceremonies.

4. Figuratively, in the Middle Ages, prison frequently denoted the body. *MED* cites instances of this use: for example, Chaucer's *Parson's Tale* I.344; *Orcherd of Syon* 355/14; and *Speculum Christiani* (2) 48/20. But for prison standing for this life, see also Chaucer's *Knight's Tale* A.3061: "Arcite ... Departed is ... Out of this foule prisoun of this lyf."

5. Erven M. Resnick, "Risus Monasticus", *Revue Benedictine* 97 (1987), 95.

6. Resnick 92.

7. Resnick 92.

8. See "The Laughing Jesus", in John Dart, *The Laughing Savior* (New York, Harper and Row, 1976). "Most Gnostics apparently believed that Jesus did not suffer on the cross inasmuch as he was in the body only as long as he wished. They claimed that at the last moment Jesus deceived his ignorant enemies and laughed at their blindness." (p. 107). Also: "Yet another Old Testament image is important here. The figure of Wisdom ('Sophia') in Proverbs has been cited by Bultmann as a key to the Gnostic redeemer concept. Once residing with God on high, Wisdom comes down to earth and attempts to spread her knowledge. She warns those who scorn her that she will laugh at and mock them when calamity comes." (p. 109). Julian associates Christ with the figure of Wisdom, but since she does not see Christ laughing, she does not apply to him the concept drawn from Proverbs.

9. Exposition on the Book of Psalms in *Nicene and Post-Nicene Fathers of the Christian Church*, ed. Philip Schaff (New York, Charles Scribner's Sons, 1917) 7: 2–3.

10. In the legend of St. Cecilia the holy woman scorns her foe Almachius and teaches her foster children how to confound the fiend with laughter.

11. Ambrose, Letter 14, 7, in *Nicene and Post-Nicene Fathers of the Christian Church* (New York and London, Parker and Co., 1896) 10, 446.

12. Louis Richard, *The Mystery of Redemption* (Baltimore and Dublin: Helicon, 1959) 9.

13. Expositions on the Psalms in *The Nicene and Post-Nicene Fathers*, ed. Philip Schaff (New York, Charles Scribner's Sons, 1917) 7:3 (on Psalm 2).

14. Psalm 2, p. 3.

15. Psalm 2, p. 3.

16. Quoted from *De Moribus* of St. Anselm, by Guy Mansini, "St. Anselm," "Satisfactio" and "The Rule of St. Benedict." *Revue Benedictine* 97 (1987), 101–121. Mansini shows that this position is consistent with the Rule of St. Benedict.

# III

# HOW DOES JULIAN BEHOLD REALITY?

## JULIAN BEHOLDS CREATION

### The Hazelnut Image

Julian's "mind is a crucible in which ideas and influences from without are fused into something wholly her own."[1]

When we look closely, we find in her texts an under-current—a subtext, we say today—of previous understandings which radically evolve with her experience.

The subject of creatures—of all that God made and pre-serves—underwent such an evolution. First she marvels at how deeply God is involved in creation. Second, she considers this truth in view of sin, of the wretchedness of all the living, and of the evil that challenges the good. And third, she develops her own classification of creatures, which gradually unfolds throughout the text.

### "All That Has Been Made"

One of the parts of the *Revelation of Love* most widely known and loved is what is generally called the hazelnut vision. She saw a small thing in the palm of her hand and learned that it is "all that has been made" (LT 5).

But before disclosing the hazelnut mystery, she invokes another image, saying:

In this same time our Lord showed me a spiritual sight
of his homely loving. I saw that he is everything that
is good and comfortable for us. He is our clothing that
for love wraps us and surrounds us for tender love, that
he may never leave us, being to us all things that are
good, as I understood it" (LT 5).

The context of this part of the first showing is the spiritual
sight of the love of God manifested in our experience of
what is good in familiar ways.

God is our clothing—in closeness to us and in comfort.
The metaphor further signifies the reality that God is also the
one who clothes us, remaining with us forever, and enfolding
and enclosing us "for tender love" (LT 5). God's "homeliness",
therefore, connotes not only intimacy, but gentleness, too.
We are thereby encouraged to trust. Related to this insight
are the scriptural lines about God's enrobing of the flowers, in
a passage also exhorting to trust: "Notice how the flowers grow.
They do not toil or spin. But I tell you, not even Solomon in
all his splendour was dressed like one of them" (Luke 12:27).

The image is a favoured one with other mystics. St. John
of the Cross, for example, in the spirit of the *Canticle*, hears
the creatures saying:

> Showering a thousand graces
> he came hurriedly through these groves,
> he looked at them and in
> the radiance of his gaze
> he left the woodland *robed* in beauty.[2]

Julian's image is more inclusive than John's and carries
a further symbolism, closer to what is human. The anchoress
in her enclosure ceremony was clothed in black garments
denoting death and repentance. But in her vision Julian is

clothed by God in comfortable clothing, suggesting God's goodness. It is significant that clothing is generic here, however, without any specific characteristics to denote ranking or degree and hence contrary to what was common in medieval society. If there is any suggestion of a type of clothing, it is that of the infant, wrapped, swaddled and enfolded by the mother, connoting love and protection.

Creatures, in Julian's view, are positive realities revealing God. Since in this first showing it was God's "homely loving" that astounded her most, it is fitting that she express this in a most ordinary sign—the putting on of comfortable clothes (LT 5). Here again she is simplifying the customs of the anchoresses, who, like the priest at the altar, were expected to make a ritual of the putting on of garments, by praying over each piece of clothing to obtain a specific virtue. Julian would have had little more than a coarsely-woven robe to draw around her; and she would have seen infants, brought to her off-street window, wrapped up warmly by loving mothers. This is an example of "homely loving"—intimate, familiar, gentle. The mother is the epitome of "homely loving".

This context establishes Julian's insight that God not only gives us what is good but is acting within creatures: for he is the goodness of whatever is.

We can appreciate Julian's originality by contrasting her clothing image with that of Walter Hilton, roughly her contemporary. For him our bodily condition denotes that we are bestial, a condition which we must reform:

By this wretchedness that I feel in myself—much more than I know how to say—I am the more able to tell you of your own image, for we all come of Adam and Eve, clad in clothes of beasts' hide, as holy scripture says of our Lord: *Fecit Deus Adae et uxori ejus tunicas pelliceas.* Our Lord made clothes of beasts' hide for Adam and his wife as a sign that for his sin he was misshapen like a beast. With these bestial clothes we are all born, wrapped up and disfigured from our natural shape.[3]

Julian sounds a different note. Her clothing image may even be a muted echo of the Genesis story, wherein she sees God as preparing protective clothing for our ancestors, not covering them with a degrading sign. Such is the reading of Genesis 3 proposed by a contemporary theologian, Phyllis Trible, who speaks of God as a loving tailor.[4]

Julian first sees the whole of creation without the intermingling of sin, and this approach conditions all that she afterwards says about what is created. This is the core of the experience of what is popularly known as the hazelnut vision. Actually, Julian says only that she saw a little thing—round as a ball and about the size of a hazelnut. We can imagine her, just realizing that she can again lift her arms, which in her partial paralysis have fallen to her side (ST 2), looking with wonderment at her hands, which are now under her control. Then comes the vision in her palm:

> I looked on it with the eye of my understanding and
> thought: "What might this be?" And in a general way
> I was answered thus: "It is all that is made." I marvelled
> at how it could last, for I thought it might suddenly
> fall apart, it was so small. And then I understood that
> it lasts, and will always last, because God loves it. And
> this is true for all that has being by the love of God
> (LT 5).

In this summation of all that is made, God is active as maker, lover, and keeper. The hazelnut allusion suggests that creation is not static or passive but has an active kernel of growth within it to be nourished. And the nut in turn feeds and nourishes. God loves not only Mary, the fullness of creation, not only sinners who need protection from evil, but all that has been made. Furthermore, the fact that sin is not present gives the vision an eternal dimension as well as a temporal one.

But even granting that creation is not a sign of evil—how important is it? Is it nought, and are we to distance ourselves from it by "noughting" ourselves, wiping out our awareness and avoiding pleasure? In dealing with this question, Julian engages in intricate word-play on the meanings of "nought", "nowten", and "nothing". It is clear enough that without God's sustaining power, creatures would fall to nothingness. But in what sense are we advised to "nowten"—to treat as nothing—these creatures that God so loves? Julian suggests that we may indeed find comfort in that which is made; but we should not seek our "rest"—that is, our ultimate peace— therein. We might well keep before us an image of something exceedingly small—like a hazelnut, as Julian does, or an apple seed would do. It would be foolish to seek satiety in such littleness when we naturally yearn for the All. Creatures are to be looked on as nothing, or "nowted", because they are not God, not because they are evil or despicable. They are indeed little, but they are not "non-existence". They simply cannot do for us what the one who made them can do. Unlike those who proposed a hierarchy of earthly loves, Julian simply distinguishes between that which is for our comfort and that which is for our rest—God alone.

Julian is still overflowing with the joy that possessed her when she realized, in part, that where Jesus is there is the Trinity. Appropriate here are words of the Bride in the

*Canticle of Canticles,* so dear to many mystics: "I came down to the nut garden/ to look at the fresh growth of the valley,/ To see if the vines were in bloom,/ if the pomegranates had blossomed" (Cant. 6:11). It is there that the speaker meets her lover. The little thing in which appears all that has been made reminds us, too, of the mystical symbol of the gem in which are mirrored all things.

In sum, in seeing the little thing like a hazelnut, Julian learns: that (1) all that is made is small in comparison with the vastness of God; (2) all that is made lasts by God's love, out of which love comes all that exists (as illustrated in the closeness between the clothing and the clothier—like the dancer and the dance); (3) created reality has properties by appropriation, for these are really properties of God, the one who makes it, loves it, preserves it; and (4) while we see creatures—that which is made, loved, and preserved—we do not see the maker, the lover, the preserver. For that, we wait for our "substantial oneing" with God. That "substantial oneing" is more intimate than that of our ordinary condition in which we are enfolded in protective garments, and it contrasts with it.

Besides, Julian cannot cut away utterly from creatures, because all of them lie in the palm of her hand—not in God's hand alone. We are to be partners in his good deed.

And we are a special kind of creature—made for God.

But we have no properties of our own either.

Hence, we move from the smallness of creatures, still made, loved, and preserved by God; to the insufficiency of creatures for our happiness, requiring us to "nought ourselves" by denying the vain impulse to find rest in them; to our place as a creature in view of salvation history—made for love, restored by love, and kept by love.

It is still true, of course, for Julian, too, that on the path to God one moves beyond creatures—though not as obstacles.

Julian is clear about this: When a person comes above all creatures to behold the Self, it cannot linger even there, but goes on to see God dwelling in the soul (LT 67). This is like someone who sees a kingdom belonging to a lord and is not at rest until he is able to see the lord himself (LT 67)—a theme she will more fully develop at another time.

## Even in a Sinful World?

After Julian marvelled at God's familiarity with the creature, she is astounded even more that such closeness extends to us who are sinful: "that he who was so much to be revered and so awesome will be so familiar *to a sinful creature* living in wretched flesh" (LT 4). It would be hard to overstate this difficulty. When we come face-to-face with the most wretched of the earth—in their pain and poverty; and even more, when we confront those who are wretched because of their cruelty, their hatred, their greed—then we know why Julian raises this doubt.

And certainly if we look back at the notions widespread in Julian's environment, we find quite different perceptions of God's goodness in creation. Augustine in the opening book of the *Confessions*, for example, stresses the sinful attractions of creatures while understating their goodness: God is the Creator and Governor of the universe. "Good ... is He who made me ..."; but "my sin was in this—that I looked for pleasures, exaltations, truths not in God Himself but in His creatures..."[5]

Furthermore, in puzzling over God's presence in creatures Augustine stumbles through spatial metaphors and metaphors of vessels not great enough to contain the Infinite. "My soul's house is too narrow for you to enter.";[6] "You

fill the heaven and the earth. Do they therefore contain you?
... Shall we not rather say this: everywhere you are present
in your entirety, and no single thing can contain you in your
entirety?"[7]

Striking also is the difference in the way Julian and Augustine present the child as a beloved creature of God. Julian
finds in the child a charming symbol of our relationship to
God: as the child in its dependence turns lovingly to the
mother, so we in our need are to turn trustingly to God.
But Augustine, reviewing the sins and malice of which children and youths are capable, could only extract a "sign"—
based on height—in order to make sense out of Christ's
injunction to us to become as little children: "It must, therefore, have been the *low stature* of children, O our King, which
you used as a sign of humility in the words: *of such is the
Kingdom of Heaven.*"[8]

Few of Julian's contemporaries were as positive as she was
on the place of creatures in God's plan for us. For example,
Richard Rolle (1300?-1349) strikes a primary note of contempt
for the world rather than paying tribute to its worth. In
*The Mending of Life*, when treating of creatures, he orients
his disciples on this theme: "For what shall delight him who
has disposed himself to loving Christ? ... The world itself
compels us to contempt of the world. ... And here are other
things that can move us to contempt of the world: the muta-
bility of time, the brevity of the present life, certain death
and the uncertain result of death, the stability of eternity,
the vanity of present things, and the truth of future joy."[9]

Even when speaking with less negativism, Rolle wavers
in assessing the goodness of creatures, saying: "But whatever
he [the contemplative] has he loves for the sake of God and
he loves nothing except what God wills him to love."[10] But
how does this agree with a statement a few lines later: "... such

a man loves all things for the sake of God."[11] Then there is a sharp reversal in the same chapter: "When, therefore, a man perfectly turned to Christ has despised all transitory things and has fixed himself as immovably in the single desire of the Creator as is permitted to mortals on account of the corruption of the flesh, then, without a doubt, exercising his spiritual powers in manly fashion, first he will see with his intellectual eye, as if by means of an opened door, the heavenly citizens."[12]

Rolle's view is cautious and complex—and confusing. Julian is consistent. As part of Christ's motherhood he directs our ways (LT 61). This includes making us love all that he loves, for his love, and enabling us to be pleased with him and with all his works (LT 61). For God does not despise anything that he has made, and he does not hesitate to serve us in the simplest ways that our body requires (LT 6). Our flesh is "wretched" because of its pain and suffering, not because of innate corruption. It is "wretched" because of the "great hurt" that has come to creatures by sin, so great that Julian needs to be told repeatedly that indeed "all things will be well" (LT 29).

And not only are creatures good, but within them, through Christ, there is power against evil. In the passion, and the Godhead therein, she saw that there was strength, not only for her, but for all creatures who would be saved—power against the onslaught of fiends (ST 3). This refers to the creature in its singularity, otherwise vulnerable before evil forces.

## Classification

Julian's contemporaries usually classified beings in a hierarchical mode: God, angels, men (and then women); animals; vegetables; minerals. The rationale for such divisions was the degree of participation in goodness, and the manner of reflecting the properties of the divine Trinity.[13] Some creatures are the image of the Trinity; others show traces of the Trinity. Inequalities were for the sake of the beauty and order of the whole. For Julian there is no hierarchy—only the uncreated and the created. But within the scope of the created there are different groupings, sometimes flexible, or different conditions experienced by particular creatures, according to their participation in God's love.

At times "creature" designates "all men", the corporate Adam. This is the case where it is said: the Father had compassion and pity on the falling of Adam, his best-loved creature (LT 51). But at other times Julian sees the creature in its singularity, as when she says: the Father takes no harder the falling of any creature that shall be saved than he took the falling of Adam (LT 53). And to balance any misunderstanding that might arise from the stress on the littleness of creatures, Julian notes that the human soul is made as perfect as possible—meaning here the soul as the City of God in which Christ dwells in heaven—yet it is still a creature: "In this he showed the delight that he has in the making of man's soul: for as perfect as the Father could make a creature, and as perfect as the Son knew how to make a creature, so perfect the Holy Ghost wanted man's soul to be made; and so it was done" (LT 67). Yet she never loses sight of human finitude, for even our substance, our closest link to God, is only a creature: God is God and our substance is a creature of God (LT 54).

Then Julian sees the grouping of individuals among "all men": speaking of them in relation to their place in God's love. For example, "the creature that sees and feels the working of love by grace hates nothing but sin" (LT 52). Then there are "those creatures who have given themselves to serve God by the inward beholding of his blessed goodness" (LT 76). She seems to behold herself as a member of this community, though at the beginning she presents herself only as a simple creature who was unlettered and who desired to love God more by experiencing the approach of death (LT 2). When the visions come she speaks of herself as "the wretched creature" to whom these insights were granted. Gradually she expresses a feeling of empowerment from God's love. Though in the vision of God in a point no work of the creature was shown, only God in the creature, she later learned, as we have seen, to be a partner in God's good deeds (LT 34). When in the tenth revelation she learns—in the vision of the cloven heart—the meaning of the words, "Lo, how I loved thee," it is as "his creature" that her understanding is enlightened (LT 24).

But Julian never overstates what creatures can comprehend. How much God loves us surpasses the knowing of creatures (LT 6). No creature that is made—does this not also include Mary?—can comprehend how much, how sweetly, and how tenderly God loves us (LT 6). All that Julian can say is that in grace and virtue Mary exceeds that of all creatures (LT 6). By this does Julian mean all creatures cumulatively, and not just any other one creature? Probably so.

In the passing reference to the king who treats his servant like kin, the servant is "a poor creature" who asks—without him being able to answer, "What more could he [the kindly king] do" for such a one? (LT 7).

Also there are those creatures who reject God's love and then repent: "I saw deadly sin in the *creatures* that will not die for their sin but live in the joy of God without end" (LT 76).

To be among the damned is another condition which creatures may choose. But Julian is counselled not to think about them. They are wiped out of all memory. She sees none of these. But in denying that she saw the damned, she indirectly reveals that she did see souls that love and fear God: "The Lord showed me no souls but those that fear him" (LT 76). We know she saw the soul of Mary. But she does not tell us what other souls she saw. Those in heaven? More likely those she counselled, who came to her hating sin, not dwelling on the pain of hell, and truly taking the teaching of the Holy Ghost.

*The Blessed Creatures*: By this category Julian refers to what she calls the "fair creation"—that creation which has reached, or is destined for, its full potential in Christ. The "fair creatures" are thus without blemish or imperfection.

She mentions these blessed creatures in the sixth revelation, wherein the Lord's banquet for his servants and friends is described: "All the blessed creatures that are in heaven shall see that worshipful thanking" at the Lord's joyful banquet. "The blessed creatures that will be in heaven: he will have them like to himself in all things" (LT 77). An example of "the fair creature" is shown to her in the vision of the little child who springs out of a body beset with wretchedness and filth to become "a full fair creature"—a new creation, not a disembodied soul (LT 64).

The blessed creatures are a wider category than humanity— and may include angels, though Julian does not see any angels in her showings. This may be surprising inasmuch as the story of St. Cecilia, which had inspired her youthful prayer, is structured around the miraculous appearances of angels—to Valerian and to Tiburtius. She does, however, refer to angels, saying that our Lord shows us no more blame than he would if we were as "pure and as holy as the angels in heaven" (LT 50). She names Gabriel in connection with the annunciation to Mary (LT 4). She thus affirms her belief in angels, but she seems to give to Christ and his members the functions of ministries which scholars had assigned to heavenly hierarchies: "He is nearest and most meek, highest and lowest, and does all" (LT 80). She speaks also of how creatures will feel on the last day of earthly time, when they will tremble and quake while the heavens also tremble and quake (LT 75).

*Creatures in the Passion*: It is in connection with the passion that Julian most fully suggests her view of creatures. In the vision of Mary at the foot of the cross, Julian understands that there is a natural love of the creature for God—exemplified in the mother-love of Mary: "In this I saw a substance of natural love, furthered by grace, which *creatures* have for him; a natural love which was most abundantly shown in his sweet mother ..." (LT 18). In the context of this showing Julian speaks of creatures more inclusively—beyond the human category. All creatures made for our service suffered with Christ at the crucifixion. She names the firmament and the earth, which grew dark for sorrow at the time of his dying—because it is in their nature "to know him for their God" (LT 18). When he failed—lost strength—it was appropriate for them, too, because of their links with him by nature, also to fail, out of sorrow for his pain. "The planets and the elements that work by nature for the blessed man and for the outcast" failed to do so at the time of Christ's death (LT 18).

It is in relation to the eighth showing that Julian presents this insight. In that showing she receives most abundantly the experience she had asked for in prayer: "The showing of Christ's pains filled me full of pain; I knew that Christ suffered only once; but he would show it to me, and fill my mind with it, as I had desired before" (LT 17). But she receives more: she perceives a great oneness which exists between Christ and us, who are creatures (LT 18). She then shows two ways in which creatures suffered at the crucifixion (Matt. 27:45–56). Both imply a sense of connectedness of all things in the Incarnate God. This sense of oneness—a truly mystical experience of the connectedness of all things—has two aspects. It affects classes of creatures in differing ways— connectedness by love and connectedness by nature.

One of these comes home to her as a development of receiving this vivid experience of the passion as she had heretofore desired—but with abundance. Mary, and all Christ's disciples and true lovers, suffered for love: that is, they were so united with him in love that even the least of them loved him surpassingly above themselves (LT 18). This is her own experience, too.

But there is another way in which creatures suffer in unity with the passion. Those who could not suffer for love because they did not know him suffered nonetheless from the disturbance in all creation. Here Julian refers to what the Gospels narrate: there was darkness over the earth, an earthquake rent the temple from top to bottom, and the rocks were split open (Matt. 27). God who is everything that is "good and comfortable" to us (LT 5) was absent: those who knew not Christ suffered "for the lack of comfort" in those creatures they had taken for granted; but they did experience God's "secret keeping"—for they did not themselves die in this terror.

She mentions two sub-divisions of people in this category, represented by Pilate and St. Denys. Her contemporaries would have given her a harsh picture of Pilate—a man who met Christ face to face, heard his claim to kingship, and ignored his wife's testimony that he was about to put to death a just man, but in the end did not know him. Julian, however, passes him by. On the other hand, she develops a portrait of St. Denys, who represents those who desired to know the living God though they knew not Christ.[14] But Julian presents St. Denys further as a symbol of mysticism alongside the Christian experience. He knows the connectedness of all that exists and interprets the cosmic disturbance as related to God.

In fact, Julian appears here to learn not only from Christ's lovers but also from this unknown mystic who does not know Christ.

Christian piety tended to consider the events narrated in connection with the crucifixion as miraculous. They were seen as a break with nature designed to give witness to the divinity of Christ. Again, reversing the trends of such piety, Julian roots this disturbance in nature itself, which is so connected in kind that it, too, suffers with the dying Christ. She enunciates a principle which does not rest on miracles: "The firmament, the earth, failed out of sorrow in their nature at the time of Christ's dying; for by nature it belongs to them to know him for their God, in whom all their strength stands; and when he failed, it was expedient for them, according to the nature of kind, to fail with him as much as they could, out of sorrow for his pains" (LT 18). And on the human side: "When he was in pain, we were in pain, and all creatures that could suffer pain suffered with him" (LT 18). This passage is not easy to interpret. But obviously it is not a time-bound, purely historical view for "we" were not literally there.

These are mysterious sayings, lacking the clarity that Julian's explanations about the crucifixion carry elsewhere. She has, indeed, gone beyond using "creature" to designate only the human being. Since she says elsewhere—and the medieval world held this generally—that humanity is a microcosm in which all other beings are caught up and given their purpose she may mean simply this: "of all natures that he has placed in various beings in part, in man is all the whole in fullness" (LT 62). This is eminently true of Jesus Christ, for "all the gifts that God may give to creatures he has given to our Lord Jesus for us" (LT 55).

This explanation might do, except for the evident allusions in her text to the account in the Scriptures where it is said that the sun and the moon were darkened when the Saviour died. She is elaborating on this account when she adds that all creation failed in giving comfort to humanity.

Is Julian's commentary prophetic, suggesting to us what can happen to all of nature if we destroy the body of Christ? Is it in the tradition of St. Francis, who spoke of brother sun and sister moon; and of the Celtic hermits who—at least in legend—saw all creation as children of God? Or is it in the tradition of Augustine who said that creatures know their God? In explaining: "for the world was made by Him, and the world knew Him not", Augustine draws a distinction: the "lovers of the world" do not know God, but creatures of the natural world do know him and bear witness to him. Augustine cites events, including the darkening of the world during the crucifixion, to show that creatures give testimony to their God:

> For did not the creature acknowledge its Creator? The
> heavens gave testimony by a star; the sea gave
> testimony, and bore its Lord when He walked upon
> it; the winds gave testimony, and were quiet at His
> bidding; the earth gave testimony, and trembled when
> He was crucified.[15]

Whether this is poetry or mysticism in Augustine is not clear. But Julian goes beyond the claim that creatures bear witness to their Lord, to say further that creatures of the natural world suffered for their Lord out of compassion. Did she mean this even in her own case, for example, when at the beginning of her experience she "wanted all *creatures* to suppose that she had died"?

What is more likely is that Julian, either in fact or in sympathy, had that closeness to nature which was the special heritage of the recluse.[16]

Is she speaking in the spirit now known through the writings of Teilhard de Chardin, who presents for us a cosmic Christ, seeing the Incarnation as bringing blessing on all matter, which is evolving towards consciousness?

In any case, it is unlike Julian to offer us merely a poetic fantasy, designed to deepen our feelings for the dying Christ. She is too realistic for that. She does speak of miracles in another context, but this event is not for her a miracle in the ordinary sense. It can, therefore, be understood as the full cycle of redemption, not as literally an historic event. Given her pattern of speaking simultaneously of time, of the consummation of time, and of eternity, she is not out of harmony with the symbolic reading of this Gospel account. The earthquake is a symbol of the resurrection of the just, compressing the event of the death of Christ with the event to come—the rising of the dead.[17]

Her explicit discussion of miracles is also in relation to her concept of creatures (LT 36). She says that God gave her "a special understanding and teaching about the working of miracles". She is reflecting on ways in which our Lord works in us: he works in us to deflect us from judging others or from giving thought to those who may be damned. Earlier she had cited miracles shown around the body of St. John Beverly, who would have been judged harshly during his life, though his contrition brought him to greater heavenly joy than he would have had if he had not fallen (LT 38).[18] She makes clear that God does these miracles, in witness to the glory the saint achieved through contrition. The purpose of the miracles here is to teach us how, in this case, the evil of sin was countered by good.

The creature will seem to have some part in the great deed which will make all things well—but what God will do "with regard to his poor creatures" she does not know (LT 36). But it is God who works miracles (though Julian's contemporaries attributed them at times to the saints as a witness to their holiness). Was this not the purpose of the miracles worked by or in witness to St. Cecilia in the legend, such as her escape from the flaming bath? The story is built around miracles. But the rationale of those miracles does not correspond at all to the analysis of miracles Julian offers, which is in four parts:

1) God is the source of many great miracles: high and marvellous, glorious and splendid; done in the past, done now, and to be done in the future.

2) Before miracles come, there is sorrow, anguish, and tribulation. Through these the creature realizes keenly its limitations—its weakness and the trouble it has got into by sin, so that it calls for help as the child runs to its mother and fears God.

3) Then miracles come—from the Trinity, in its might, wisdom, and goodness. They come to show God's power, to show the joys of heaven so far as is possible here on earth, and to strengthen our faith and hope, in charity.

4) God is pleased to be acknowledged and known in miracles, for these reasons just given (LT 36).

Julian's simple teaching on miracles is singularly enlightened and not as centrally focused on power as was that of spiritual writers before her. She is also more mystical, and less moralizing in her view of such interventions. Augustine taught that whereas God's action in nature signifies his presence, in miracles it signifies his power.[19] Augustine was also among those who emphasized the moral impact expected from miracles: when effects that we call "natural" are brought about by an unusual change, in order to teach men some lesson, then they are called miracles.[20] Julian goes beyond these reasons and sees miracles also as a foretaste of heavenly joys, as an act of divine self-disclosure, as a comfort to us in our distress, and a motive for reverential fear.

St. Thomas had classified miracles in three degrees: 1) works done by God which nature could never do; 2) works which nature can do but not in the same order—as when a man walks after having been lame; and 3) works in which God does what nature can do but without the means of natural principles—as when a man is suddenly cured of a fever.[21] Julian speculated that her instantaneous cure from fever and paralysis was of this type: "I marvelled at this sudden change for I thought it came from the secret working of God and not of nature" (LT 3). In this change she particularly saw God's goodness at work.

Her only examples of miracles are this instantaneous healing, the events attesting to the holiness of the saints, and the action of the creatures at the crucifixion revealing what will happen at the resurrection. All these manifest, not so much God's power, as divine compassion.

All in all, this section on miracles is a digression, and after it Julian returns to a simpler way of speaking of creatures. Her view of creatures, and our part in what they do, is important. A price has been paid for the religious legacy that taught the despising of creatures. For if we despise creatures, and consider ourselves altogether separate from them, the horror and terror of nature, and even more of society, can go on unchecked by the energies of religious persons. But since the human soul has the same properties in created form as the Trinity in uncreated form, we are expected to work in seeing Truth, leading by Wisdom, and delighting in Love.

All this she draws out from the vision of a small, round thing, like a hazelnut, in the palm of her hand, which is now restored to health and potential for writing, comforting, gesturing, restoring the garments of the poor.

The *Cloud* author had taught his disciple to place all creatures under a cloud of forgetting and try—if possible—even to abstract from the fact of his own being. The exercise was intended to bring him into contact with God as love. Julian also offers an exercise in forgetting, but it is quite different (ST 20). Hers is an exercise designed to help us understand how we are individually and personally loved.

The exercise is described in the short text where she says that God would have done everything that he has done for her alone: "And everyone should think this, knowing God's love, and forgetting so far as possible all other creatures, thinking that God has done for me all that he has done" (ST 20). The exercitant reviews and keeps in mind the beneficence of God in singular ways, knowing that his love is not dispersed or diluted because it touches many. But this reflection is not an end in itself—lest it deteriorate into ego-centredness. It is a step in a process. This exercise, she says, should move a person to love God, to be pleased with God, and not to fear. In this context, too, Mary is the prime example of this singular loving: "Will you see in her how you are loved?" (LT 25). And always related to this insight is Julian's assurance in a later context where she affirms that the great deed which will bring the destiny of corporate humanity to fulfilment "does not exclude the individual" (LT 36).

Such is the balance Julian maintains between creaturehood

corporatively and singly. We are singularly loved, and creatures are for our service and comfort, but not for our rest, not to quiet the questing human desires. Julian's perspective on creaturehood is always comprehensive—sweeping in one glance from the gift of existence, through the change wrought by the passion, to the new creation that will endure forever. It is always in view of the great deed.

## *Endnotes*

1. Andrew Louth, "The Influence of Denys the Areopagite on Eastern and Western Spirituality in the Fourteenth Century", *Sobornost* 4 (1982), 185–200 (esp. p. 190).
2. *Respuesta de las criaturas*: Mil gracias derramando,/pasó por estos sotos con presura,\y yéndolos mirando,\con sola su figura/*vestidos*; los dejó de herm∴sura. *The poems of St. John of the Cross*, English Versions and Introduction by Willis Barnstone (New York, New Directions Books, 1972) 92–93.
3. *Stairway of Perfection*, trans. John P.H. Clark and Rosemary Dorward (New York, Paulist Press, 1991) Bk I, chap. 84, 154.
4. Phyllis Trible, *God and the Rhetoric of Sexuality* (Philadelphia, Fortress Press, 1980) 134.
5. Augustine, *The Confessions of St. Augustine*, trans. Rex Warner (New York, New American Library, 1963) Bk. I.20, 39.
6. *Confessions*, Bk. I.5, p. 20.
7. *Confessions*, Bk. I.4, p. 18.
8. *Confessions*, Bk. I.20, p. 38.
9. *Fire of Love and the Mending of Life*, trans. M.L. del Mastro (Garden City, N.Y., Doubleday & Co., 1981) Chap. 1, pp. 50–51.
10. *Fire of Love* Chap. 19, 163.
11. *Fire of Love* Chap. 19, 163.

12. *Fire of Love* Chap 19, 165.
13. Thomas Aquinas argued that creatures were distinguished by matter and form. Each angel exhausts the perfection of its species and therefore there is no multiplication of the species. But "in natural things species seem to be arranged in a degrees; as the mixed things are more perfect than the elements, and plants than minerals, and animals than plants, and men than other animals; and in each of these one species is more perfect than the others. Therefore, as the divine wisdom is the cause of the distinction of things for the sake of the perfection of the universe, so it is the cause of inequality. For the universe would not be perfect if only one grade of goodness were found in things."

    Aquinas also distinguishes creatures according to image and trace—that is, as to the manner in which they reflect the Trinity. "... in rational creatures, possessing intellect and will, there is found the representation of the Trinity by way of image, inasmuch as there is found in them the word conceived in the intellect and the love proceeding" (ST I.I, quest. 45, art. 7, corpus): "But in all creatures there is found the trace of the Trinity, inasmuch as in every creature are found some things which are necessarily reduced to the Divine Persons as to their cause. For every creature subsists in its own being; it has a form by which it is determined to a species, and has relation to something else." (ST I.I, quest. 47, art. 2. corpus).

14. "We are reminded that 'St. Denys of France' is meant to be Dionysius the Areopagite (temple-keeper) who is depicted in Acts 17:34 as having been converted by St. Paul at Athens. The Acts, of course, does not mention anything at all about Dionysius except to give his name, in the one verse. Popular medieval piety, however, knew him as a theologian and he was a symbol of the pagans who desired to worship the True God, although they were ignorant of Christ." Pelphrey, *Love Was His Meaning*, 263.

15. "On the Gospel of St. John," Tractate III, 5 in *Nicene and Post-Nicene Fathers*, ed. Philip Schaff (New York, Charles Scribner's Sons, 1908) 7:20.

16. Jean Leclercq, "Solitude and Solidarity", in *Peace Weavers*, ed. John A. Nichols and Lillian Thomas Shank (Kalamazoo, Mich.: Cistercian Publications, Inc., 1987) 71.

17. For a similar interpretation see notes on Matt. 27: 51-53, in *The Catholic Study Bible*, (New York, Oxford University Press, 1990) 63.

18. Biographies of St. John Beverly do not record that he lived a sinful life, however.

19. See *De Trinitate*. Bk. 3, chaps. 4-5, in *The Trinity*, trans. Stephen McKenna (Washington, D.C., Catholic University of America Press, 1963) 105-106. For a study on miracles see Benedicta Ward, *Miracles and the Medieval Mind* Theory, Record and Event 1000-1215 (Philadelphia: University of Pennsylvania Press, 1982, 1987), especially chaps. I, II, and IX. See also John A. Hardon, S.J., "The Concept of Miracle from St. Augustine to Modern Apologetics," *Theological Studies* 15 (1954): 229-57.

20. *De Trinitate*. Bk. 3, chap. 6, in *The Trinity*, trans. Stephen NcKenna (Washington, D.C., Catholic University of America Press, 1963) 107.

21. *Summa Contra Gentiles*, Chap. 101, in *Basic Writings of Thomas Aquinas*, ed. Anton C. Pegis (New York, Random House, 1945) 2: 198-99.

# MARY, FULLNESS OF CREATION

Julian wrote in a context in which all theological doctrines, including doctrines on Mary, were articulated almost entirely by men. Literary men, in turn, both reflected these doctrines and incorporated in their writings some of the beliefs of popular piety. Although these men, as well as Julian, exalted Mary, Julian did not follow them in her pattern of praise. Her portrait of Mary is original and unique, and anticipates a recognition of Mary's universal motherhood, which did not appear officially in the Church until quite modern times.

For instance, Julian distinguishes herself from the popular piety of her age which regarded Mary as "an omnipotent suppliant" and as a quasi-legal advocate for helpless sinners. The Saint Bernard of Dante's *Paradiso* cautions that anyone who desires grace and does not pray to Mary is like a person trying to fly without wings. In a Chaucerian translation a French poet prays to be protected by Mary against God's wrath: "Help that my Father be not wroth with me." And "Who shall unto thy Son my mene [mediator] be? Who, but thyself, that art the well of pity?"[1] In Julian's view these appeals are unnecessary, for Christ already loves us. Instead of being an indispensable mediator, Mary is a model of the creation which God endlessly loves.

Both Dante and Chaucer had indicated that the Son of God did not disdain to become human because human nature in Mary was so ennobled. But such praise of Mary was often the occasion of implying that the rest of creation was to be despised. For example, the Second Nun in the *Canterbury Tales* laments the contagion of the body in which the soul is imprisoned, along with the burden of earthly desires and disordered affections. Such is not Julian's position. Rather, she sees the world as the work of God's goodness in which we are all called to collaborate. In this view Mary is the paradigm of those who work to manifest that goodness.

A favourite title for Mary in Julian's day was "the new Eve", who brings life to the world, in contrast to the First Eve, who brought death. This idea developed in the twelfth century into the notion of Mary's "spiritual motherhood". She acquires this "spiritual motherhood" on Calvary, where all are her adopted children, as represented by John. But Julian did not see Mary's role as simply parallel to that of Mother Eve: Mary's role is more complex. Her motherhood, in Julian's vision, is not merely metaphorical, nor her children "adopted". Rather, she is the real and literal mother of the whole Christ, including all those incorporated into him.

While Julian's portrait of Mary in the *Showings* thus stands apart from many of these ways in which she was enshrined in medieval popular piety, her starting-point was a favoured one. It was her desire to see a vivid representation of the crucifixion, with Mary standing near in deep compassion: "I desired a bodily sight wherein I might better know the bodily pains of our Saviour and the compassion of Our Lady ..." (LT 2). This petition was fulsomely granted: "I had sight of the passion of Christ in a number of showings: in the first, the second, the fifth, and the eighth ... whereby I had in part a feeling of the sorrow of our Lady and of his true friends who saw him in pain ..." (LT 33).

## Mary as the Fullness of Creation

Though Julian's first vision was of Christ crowned with thorns, she did not, initially, see Mary in her sorrow near the cross. Rather, she first saw her in the context of the whole of creation, as understood in the hazelnut vision, in which Julian "saw not sin". In that showing Mary appeared as a young girl, in a form more spiritual than embodied, and slight in stature, as she was at the time she conceived. Through the one whom she bears within her, all that has been made will become a new creation.

Mary is herself the fullness of creation, above everything except the humanity of her Son. What the work of creatures is in fulfilling that creation was disclosed in that first showing in the soul of Mary. In her as the perfect exemplar was the Truth, Wisdom, and Love which is God, at work in the creature, and with the help of the creature. The ground of meekness is to realize, as Mary did, that one has all by creation and divine keeping, nothing of oneself (LT 44).

In her archetypal role, Mary is the "fair kind"—humanity as it is meant to be and will be when restored by the passion: "she [Mary] was fulfilled in grace and in all manner of virtues" (LT 7). Hence, it is fitting to petition God "for love of the sweet mother who bore him" (LT 6). Such a practice, however, can be misdirected through "lack of understanding and knowing of love" (LT 6). But so long as we address ourselves basically to the goodness of God, we are expected to use the means which have been given us. And the first means we are to use is the blessed nature of Christ which he "took from the maid" (LT 6).

Yet access to God requires no special messenger, though we regard as God's gift the love and friendship of Mary and of all the saints. Furthermore, when Mary says, "Behold me, God's handmaid" (LT 4), she opens the path for us, too, to be partners with God "in his good deed" (LT 43). In Julian's view the "good deed" is the fullest manifestation of God's goodness.

By this stress on the goodness of God, Julian is laying the groundwork for her teaching that Christ is our true mother. Goodness, she says, is that property in God which does good against evil. And in a deliberate parallel: "Thus Jesus Christ who does good against evil is our true mother" (LT 59). Likewise in this very first showing, Julian further prepares for the theme of the motherhood of Christ by listing the deeds that flow from the property of goodness. The language in this description will be echoed when she speaks of Christ as mother. In the first showing she says:

We are enclosed in the goodness of God. . . . It quickens our soul, brings it to life, and makes us to grow in grace and virtue. It is closest to us in nature and it is the most prompt to bring us grace. It is that grace which we seek now and always, until we know that we are enfolded in God. For God has no disdain for creation nor no aversion for serving us in the simplest offices that pertain to our bodies . . . . It is more worship to God that . . . we pray to the divine goodness (LT 6).

In her chapters on the motherhood of Christ, Julian presents parallel points:

Thus Jesus is truly our mother in kind (nature), in our first making (LT 59). . . . The mother's service is closest, most prompt, and surest, for it is most true (LT 60). . . . As the child changes in age, the mother relaxes her working but not her love (LT 60). . . . As the child increases in age she permits that it be chastised for the breaking down of vices to make it receptive to virtues and graces (LT 60). . . . All the sweet kindly office of motherhood is proper to the second person (LT 59). . . . It behoves us to love our God from whom we have our being . . . praying mightily to our mother of grace and pity (LT 59).

Julian goes so far as to say that the very motive of the Incarnation was to extend the motherhood of the Word, and that such was the teaching of the first revelation:

Our kind mother [Christ], our gracious mother, because he would be our mother in all things, took the ground of his working full low and full mildly in the maiden's womb; and he showed that in the first revelation where he brought before the eye of my understanding that

86

meek maid, in simple stature as she was when she conceived (LT 60).

The core disclosure of the first showing is that the thorn-crowned Jesus is God, and where Jesus appears, there is the Trinity. We look on Jesus, and there is the Trinity. This is parallel—but not identical—with the revelation about Mary. We look into her soul, and there is an image of the Wisdom and Truth of that same Trinity. Mary in this way mirrors the motherhood by which Divine Wisdom brings all that has been made to the fullness it was meant to have from the beginning, and more—just as if sin had never been. As Julian beholds these mysteries, she is filled with overflowing love for her even-Christians.

## *Mary as All Creation, Longing for God*

In the second showing Julian gains an insight, through beholding Mary at the foot of the cross, as to how all creatures, even the earth itself, are moved by compassion and longing for God. This was the vision Julian had prayed for, along with the desire to feel contrition, compassion, and a longing for God. The first vision revealed how Mary manifests creation at its fullest. The second shows in her compassion how creation longs for God and finds fruition in God.

Mary is the good earth—fertile, flowering and fruitful, whereon the seed of the divine Word falls. The disfigured face of Christ, born of the human mother, is the same face that will be transformed in heaven: "the blessed face which is the beauty of heaven, the flower of the earth, the fruit of the maiden's womb" (LT 10).

Not in Mary alone, but in the whole earth, there is sorrow at the disfigurement of Christ's face and the dying of God:

"The firmament, the earth, grew weak for sorrow—each according to its kind—at the time of Christ's dying. ... for sorrow at his pains" (LT 18). "I saw the substance of that natural love, continued by grace, which all creatures have for him—a love shown most abundantly in his dear mother" (LT 18). Mary is in solidarity with the whole of creation. Yet because her love was greatest, Mary suffered most and most perfectly showed compassion. Like Mary all creatures, in their own degrees, long in the depth of their natures for their Maker, the ground of their being and the source of all goodness.

*Mary, a Sign of How We Are Loved:* In the eleventh showing Mary still stands by the cross, but the vision is of her blessed state in heaven. The lesson of this showing is how God loves us. Mary is a link between God and us by having made it possible for Christ to be one with us in human suffering: though our salvation is the work of the whole Trinity, "only the maiden's son suffered" (LT 23). In his wounded side Christ reveals the joy to come: it was "a fair, delightful place, large enough for all humanity to rest in peace and love" (LT 24). It is the city of God, the heavenly Jerusalem, our mother.

With an expression "of mirth and joy our good Lord looked down on the right side and brought to mind where our Lady stood at the time of the passion" (LT 25). "Our Lady, Saint Mary" is revealed at this time, not sorrowing, but rejoicing in heaven, high, noble, glorious, and full of joy (LT 25). Julian is taught not to long to see her bodily but rather to find joy in how God loves her.

Christ instructs Julian to see in Mary how much each of us is loved—how the whole city of God is loved (LT 25). In consequence, all who love God are called upon to take delight in Mary, God's own beloved. For, if a man love a creature singularly above all other creatures, he will make all to love and take delight in that one whom he loves so much (LT 25). Christ's willing acceptance of the cross is a sign of his love for Mary, too, and she owes to him all that she received. This signifies that it was not payment for sin that sent Christ to the cross but a love that ended in the cross because of the sinfulness of the human condition. His love for Mary is not lost in some vague, generalized love for the whole community of the blessed. He loves her—and us—as individuals. For Julian can say: "If there were no soul on earth except one, he would be with it, all alone, until he had brought it to bliss" (LT 80). In one sense, of course, all the children of salvation are one soul. This provides Julian with a prime motive for loving each one: "What can make me to love my even-Christians more than to see in God that he loves all who are to be saved as though they were one soul?" (LT 37).

*A Sign of the City of God:* But Mary is also a symbol of the city of God. She re-enters Julian's contemplation in the thirteenth showing. This showing helps us to see how all things shall be well, given the fact of sin which has caused such sorrow. Mary's role in redemption is woven into the telling of the parable of the Lord and the Servant. An eager servant sent out by his lord on a journey falls painfully to the earth. The servant is in one sense Adam and all of humanity, and in an interlocking sense the Christ-Adam and redeemed humanity. While Adam falls into the chaotic earth, Christ falls into the good earth, the womb of Mary: "He starts out willingly and anon he falls low into the maiden's womb" (LT 51). Then in fuller detail:

Adam fell from life to death into the abyss of this wretched world and after that into hell. God's Son [the perfect Adam] fell with Adam into the abyss of the

89

womb of the maiden—that fairest daughter of Adam—
and for the purpose of excusing Adam from blame in
heaven and on earth (LT 51).

Repeatedly, in the same chapter Julian, as in a refrain, includes
Mary in her account of the servant. For example:

The starting out of the servant [Christ] was the godhead;
and the running was the manhood. *For the Godhead
starts out from the Father into the maiden's womb, falling
into the taking of our kind, our nature.* . . . The hurt that
he took was our flesh in which he felt such mortal pains
(LT 51).

Now that this teaching on the role of Mary as Christ's
mother has been explored, Julian is able to name Mary, too,
as our mother: "God knitted himself to our body in the
maiden's womb . . . in which oneing he was perfect man [col-
lective humanity]. For Christ having knit unto himself every
person that shall be saved, is perfect [complete] man . . . Thus
our Lady is our mother in whom we are all enclosed and
of her born in Christ; for she that is mother of our Saviour
is mother of all that shall be saved in the Saviour" (LT 57).
In other words, Mary bore all those whose life was included
in that of Christ inasmuch as his members were united to
him as their head, comprising the mystical body.

The members, God's partners (LT 43), are to do what they
can. As their head, the Christ-servant labours, like a gardener,
cultivating the chaotic earth. The Roman Rite for the feasts
of Mary makes use of this metaphor of the Christ-gardener,
in words taken from Isaiah:

As the earth brings forth its plants,
    and a garden makes its growth spring up,
So will the Lord GOD make justice and praise
    spring up before all the nations. (Is. 61:11)

But because of sin the Christ-servant endures pain in his labours: "from the time that he was fallen into the maiden's womb" he could not rise until after he was slain; and then he took with him into heaven "all humanity for whom he was sent" (LT 51).

On his return to heaven the servant is united to "the fair maiden" which is the collective person of the redeemed (LT 61). Mary is not "the new Eve", but "the fairest daughter of Adam" (LT 51), and Adam, as we saw above, is all humanity.

Then, just as the servant was both Adam and Christ, the "handmaid" is both the woman of Nazareth and the woman who signifies the company of the redeemed in heaven, "the fair maiden".

### Julian's Distinctive Doctrine

Thus Mary mirrors God's goodness in all creation: Christ's love—and the longing of creatures for God—in the communion of compassion between mother and Son; and in God's wisdom in bringing good out of evil, culminating in the bliss of heaven. She is the city of the elect, who were knit on earth to the Incarnate God whom she bore. He who once rested in her womb on earth, now rests in the new earth, the city of the elect in heaven, in bliss and joy.

So poetic and metaphorical is Julian's presentation of Mary it is easy to overlook what is distinctive in her teaching about "Our Lady". First, Julian distances herself from any suggestion of Mary as warding off God's wrath, for Julian taught that Christ loves us even as he loves Mary. This is a further reason why Julian's omission of the title "the New Eve" is consistent with the overall view in the *Showings*. Such a title would not fit in with the parable of the Lord and the Servant, for Eve, though she is the mother of the individual Adam, is not the mother of the collective Adam, and the parallel with Mary—the mother of both the man Jesus and the body of believers—breaks down. Second, Julian allows the motherhood of Christ to overshadow that of Mary herself, affirming that Christ took our flesh, entered into the human condition, to be our mother—giving birth to us and serving, leading, and teaching us as children. Third, Julian's interpretation of Mary's motherhood of humanity (often called spiritual maternity) pre-dates such a teaching in the Church's magesterium and anticipates by centuries the present doctrinal explanation of that motherhood.

The theme of spiritual motherhood was initially based on a parallel between Mary and the Church, and at times was only a metaphor.[2] The first pope to allude to the spiritual maternity of Mary was Sixtus IV in 1477—more than a half century after Julian's death. But present research has not produced any evidence to show that the sovereign pontiffs from Sixtus IV to Pius IX (1846–78) went beyond a metaphorical meaning when they taught the doctrine.[3]

Not until Pius X was the doctrine taught officially in the sense in which Julian presents it—as a reality founded in our incorporation in Christ and in the role of Mary in the Incarnation. In *Ad diem illam* (1904) Pius X writes:

Is not Mary the mother of Christ? She is therefore also my mother ... inasmuch as he [Christ] is God-Man He has a body like other men; inasmuch as He is redeemer of our race, He has a spiritual body, or, as it is called, a Mystical Body. ... But the Virgin did not conceive the Son of God only in order that, receiving from her His human nature, He might become man, but also in

order that, by means of this nature received from her,
He might become the Saviour of mankind ... thus in
the Virgin's chaste womb itself ... He joined to Himself
a spiritual Body formed of all those who were to believe
in Him; and it can be said that, bearing Jesus in her
womb, Mary bore also those whose life was included
in that of the Saviour.[4]

Thus Julian's teaching on Mary embodies authentic and
enduring themes. But it also anticipates what was not
officially taught until centuries later. That teaching encompasses Mary's place in the life of the individual believer, in
the community of faith—and in the whole of creation. It
is linked with the motherhood of Divine Wisdom, by which
evil will be turned into good, so that "all manner of things
shall be well" (LT 27).

## Endnotes

1. "An ABC", freely rendered by Chaucer from Deguilleville's
   "Pèlerinage de la Vie Humaine", in *The Works of Geoffrey
   Chaucer*, ed. F.N. Robinson, 2nd ed. (Boston, Houghton, 1957)
   525, 526: "Help that my Fader be not wroth with me. ... Who
   shal unto thi Sone my mene bee?/Who, but thiself, that art
   of pitee welle?"
2. The theme occurs in Ambrose and Augustine. Ambrose Aupert
   (d. 784) said that we can speak of both Mary and the Church
   as virgin-mother, because in Mary's womb the Church was
   united to Christ. Bede (d. 735) used similar language. Hilda C.
   Graef, *The Devotion to Our Lady*, Twentieth Century Encyclopedia of Catholicism 106 (New York, Hawthorn Books, 1963)
   21–23.
3. W.J. Cole, "Mary, Blessed Virgin, II", *New Catholic Encyclopedia*
   9: 352–4.
4. Cole 353.

# JULIAN BEHOLDS GOD

*God in a Point: "And I Saw Not Sin"*

The whole of the third showing focuses on the image: "I saw God in a point" (LT 11).

"Point" has been translated by some to mean: "in an instant of time".[1] From as far back as the pseudo-Dionysius some have taken the point to symbolize, geometrically, the philosophical concept of God as the starting centre from which creation radiates:

> ... all the radii of a circle are concentrated into a single
> unity in the centre, and this point contains all the
> straight lines brought together within itself, and unified
> to one another, and to the one starting point from
> which they began.[2]

Dante sees the point as light in God's mind, radiating out into all that is created. Others have identified the point with the mystical centre or ground of the soul—the "still point", in which ineffable, non-discursive, non-imaged knowledge of God is disclosed.[3] Certainly in Julian the point is not a measure of time nor an indicator of linear relations.

Julian's image differs from and transcends these traditional usages. The point does not connote a static centre from which creation radiates, for God is present in every particle of what is made. The point signifies the reality of God at the heart of all things. That is why, in this showing, Julian says: "I saw that he is in all things" (LT 11).

God is the central point of all, and all human life is only a point in him. God is present to the lowest part of human needs (LT 6). Julian may be thinking, then, of needle-point (or lace-point), which anchoresses made. In such a structure each point (or stitch) is everywhere the same, yet each is really distinct from the pattern which arises from the points. Also this pattern pre-exists in the mind of the worker, who, for a perfect work, never lifts her hands from what she makes. Such a metaphor conveys Julian's teaching that God is in all things, as maker and keeper, yet is really other from what he sustains in being.[4]

In addition to understanding in the showing that God is present in all things, Julian also grasps that he "is the midpoint of all things, and of all he does" (LT 11). That is, God penetrates human life—controls its destiny—from moment to moment. God is the flash of the woof-spindle shaping the texture of life's warp and woof. God is the point at which the needle produces the interstices as well as the pattern which gives beauty to the lacework. There are roots of this meaning in the derivation and cultural accretions of the word "time':

> ... the Roman peoples translated *kairos* by their word
> *tempus*, which is not only a word for "time", but also
> gives us the word, "temple". *Tempus* is the place where
> penetration is easiest, to the divine or to the body.
> Homer, for example, used *kairos* to indicate the place
> in man's body where a weapon could penetrate deepest
> for the vulnerability within ("temple" in the head). We
> might call it an "opening" or a "loophole."[5]

But given the importance of the weaving trade to Julian's city of Norwich, the meaning of *kairos* or time in that context is relevant as it images human life:

95

So also *kairos* ... meant the momentary *opening* in the warp-threads of a loom through which the woof-spindle was shot like an arrow by the expert weaver. This moment is the fateful moment, the weaving of fate and destiny. It happens at just the right time and takes a proper rhythm, hitting *between* the threads.[6]

If Julian were meditating on the flying and accurate woof spindle, she has a vivid image for saying that nothing is done by chance, but everything in the wise foresight of God.

Her image of the point is cumulative. Her pinnacle insight, shared in reflections on the thirteenth showing, is that God is the point towards which human life is tending—its final meaning:

For by the same blessed power, wisdom, and love by which he made all things, to the same end our good Lord *leads* it continually, and shall himself bring it thereto. And when it is time, we shall see it. The ground of this was shown in the first showing, and more clearly in the third, where it says: "I saw God in a point" (LT 35).

Later in the same showing, as we shall note again in the discussion of the mystery of sin, she returns to this interpretation, teaching us there that "he is with us *on earth*, *leading* us; and that was shown in the third [showing] where I saw God in a point" (LT 52). In summing up the primary modes of the revelations, she includes the image of the point: "And in another way he showed himself *on earth*, where I say: 'I saw God in a point'" (LT 81).

Here Julian's imagery is similar to that of Teilhard de Chardin. For him matter is evolving into life and consciousness and finally into fulfilment in Christ. Christ becomes the centre which gathers the whole creation into a unity:

> The point in which all matter and life and consciousness
> finds its ultimate meaning and purpose he [Teilhard de
> Chardin] calls the "Omega point". He saw the whole
> universe converging on this ultimate point, where it is
> totally unified and centred. It is towards that supreme
> point of unity that the whole creation is moving.[7]

Hence, the image of the point is multiform. It suggests (1) God present in all things. (2) God working in all things. (3) God leading humanity, during our earthly sojourn. (4) God the eternal end-point, both as meaning and as unity, towards which all creation is converging. Since sin—except as its effects are transformed—does not figure in these properties of God and creation, Julian "saw not sin" in the third showing, where nothing is amiss. In the thirteenth showing, wherein the fact of sin is uppermost, when she returns to reflect on the image of God in a point, she sees that in that final convergence-point all will be made well. God in a point is therefore both a temporal process and an eternal reality. Like a culminating note of music, which encompasses the theme of the whole, God is living in us and transcends us. In the point of the Spirit we know ourselves as open to the divine mystery, and we see that the Reality within and the Reality without are the same.

### Endnotes

1. See, for example, Colledge and Walsh, *A Book of Showings*, II, 336, note 3. This interpretation is followed by Grace Jantzen,

*Julian of Norwich, Mystic and Theologian* (New York, Paulist Press, 1987) 180.

2. Cited by Sister Anna Maria Reynolds, "Some Literary Influences in the *Revelations* of Julian of Norwich", in *Leeds Studies in English and Kindred Languages* 7–8 (1952) 24.

3. Cited by Ritamary Bradley, "Julian of Norwich: Writer and Mystic", *An Introduction to the Medieval Mystics of Europe*, ed. Paul Szarmach (Albany, State University of New York, 1984) 208.

4. Bradley, "Julian of Norwich: Writer and Mystic" 208.

5. David L. Miller, *Christs. Meditations on Archetypal Images in Christian Theology* (New York, The Seabury Press, 1981) I, 156–57.

6. Miller 157.

7. Bede Griffiths, "A New Vision of Reality", *Western Science, Eastern Mysticism and Christian Faith*, ed. Felicity Edwards (London, HarperCollins, 1989) 93.

# THE PARABLE OF THE LORD AND THE SERVANT

## (a) *The Narrative: Structure and Meaning*

The Lord and the Servant parable is Julian's way of dealing with a world where there is sin. The story is central to the meaning of the whole of the *Showings*. She had introduced the metaphor of a servant and a "noble king or great lord" in the first showing, where she touches on the relationship between the two.

To see her complex story in depth, it is helpful to examine it (1) as to subject matter; (2) in relation to what precedes her story, both in analogues and in her own text; and

(3) in its narrative content, both as allegory and as organized around the central motif of the fall.

## *Why a Parable about a Lord?*

On the surface there is little appeal in our times in a spiritual teaching which bases its symbolism on a king, a lord, and a servant. Sociologically these are tainted terms in the contemporary world. Words like these seem to posit a relationship of domination rooted in the medieval mind and in patriarchal Christian ity. Such words make us recall the bloody wars of Julian's times as struggles among kings to supplant one another.

The King of kings, however, has no need of the kingship of nations. But the point of Julian's parable still remains to be explored. For our times, too, have cases where heads of democratic entities take on the autocratic manners associated with tyrannical kings. We have seen heads of state surrounded by the pomp considered characteristic of absolute rulers. We have seen the destructive impulse towards power over others sprouting up in the most unlikely places. The image of Julian's lord is at odds with these attitudes. It is therefore a perennial parable about dealing with power, and the real meaning of the kingdom of God.

In theology, of course, it still remains true that God is the master, and we are the servants. And in Julian's story, the intent is to show the lord—and the king—not simplistically either as authority figures or as benevolent rulers, but as friends and givers of gifts, as exemplars of goodness. In the eighth showing (LT 20), Julian stresses the point that the suffering and humiliation of Christ on the cross is set in bold relief by the kingship of the Godhead. From God as king came the strength that enabled Christ to suffer so intensely. As king, God is all worthy, most deserving of being reverenced, noble, and glorious without measure. In Julian's interpretation Christ does not empty himself of the Godhead in order to become a servant, but by the strength of that Godhead becomes capable in the human order of a self-emptying that outstrips all other examples of compassion and service to others.

Julian's great parable is revolutionary for any time. Small wonder that she delayed some twenty years before attempting to explicate it.

The story is rich in Scriptural motifs: that of the Last Supper, where servants are made into friends; the gardener, who cultivates the wilderness of this world and makes us partners in his deeds; a meal symbolic of the eternal festivities. The dramatic movement reveals the theme: "I no longer call you slaves ... I have called you friends" (John 15:15); and the desire of Christ, who prayed to the Father: "that they may be one, as we are one" (John 17:22).

The immediate purpose of the parable is to present in poetic form an answer to Julian's anguished concern about blame attaching to us as sinful beings—and why sin was not prevented. This concern takes on a special poignancy in the context of a theology that often imaged God as a king taking vengeance to restore his offended honour.

## What Goes Before

*Analogues of the Parable:* In order to appreciate how nuanced and poetic Julian's parable is, we can begin with analogues of her story. One is from St. Thomas Aquinas, who depicts Christ as our brother and king. St. Anselm creates two one-dimensional stories to illustrate how God looks on us in our sin—the same problem with which Julian is concerned.

Here is St. Thomas' brief parable, which focuses on our desire to seek out Christ, so as to share in both private affection and public honours:

> Suppose . . . that there were a man who had a brother
> far away, a brother who was a king. Surely this man
> would want to go and be with his brother—because the
> brother would combine all public and private affection,
> all the good of kingdom and family. The man would
> seek out his brother, the king, in order to find him and
> abide with him. Christ is our brother and our king,
> and so we want to find him, so that we might live in
> the kingly household as subject.[1]

Anselm's first parable focuses on the servant, who is depicted as intentionally blameworthy:

> Suppose one should assign his slave a certain piece of
> work, and should command him not to throw himself
> into a ditch, which he points out to him and from
> which he could not extricate himself; and suppose that
> the slave, despising his master's command and warning,
> throws himself into the ditch before pointed out, so
> as to be utterly unable to accomplish the work assigned;
> think you then that his inability will at all excuse him
> for not doing his appointed work?[2]

Anselm's second parable tells of a king whose rebellious subjects have suffered his condemnation. This king can be appeased only by one who, because he himself is blameless, is able to satisfy the offended king, by a service which is efficacious, once and for all, for those who come before or after the day of appeasement:

For, suppose there were a king against whom all the people of his provinces had rebelled, with but a single exception of those belonging to their race, and that all the rest were irretrievably under condemnation. And suppose that he who alone is blameless had so great favour with the king, and so deep love for us, as to be both able and willing to save all those who trusted in his guidance; and this because of a certain very pleasing service which he was about to do for the king, according to his desire; and, inasmuch as those who are to be pardoned cannot all assemble on that day, the king grants, on account of the greatness of the service performed, that whoever, either before or after the day appointed, acknowledged that he wished to obtain pardon by the work that day accomplished, and to subscribe to the condition there laid down, should be freed from all past guilt; and, if they sinned after this pardon, and yet wished to render atonement and to be set right again by the efficacy of this plan, they should again be pardoned, only provided that no one enter his mansion until this thing be accomplished by which his sins are removed. In like manner, since all who are saved cannot be present at the sacrifice of Christ, yet such virtue is there in his death that its power is extended even to those far remote in place or time.[3]

Since these two parables both refer to the subject of humanity's guilt and Christ's satisfaction, they can be thought of as a single parable in two parts.

*Anticipation of the Parable in Julian's Text:* Guilt and the exacting of satisfaction are absent from Julian's story, which presents a God-image of courtesy and kindness. Julian affirms this God-image and hints at the parable itself in the first showing, when she says:

> And of all parts of the showing, what was most
> comforting to me was that our God and lord, who is
> so to be revered and held in awe, is also so familiar
> and courteous. And this was what filled me with delight
> and with a sense of security (LT 7).

The germ of the central parable is then foreshadowed, though presented in simpler terms than the fully developed one:

> And to help me understand this, he showed me this
> plain example: It is the greatest honour a majestic king
> or a great lord can pay a poor servant if he will be
> familiar with him, and especially if he makes this
> known, with complete sincerity and a pleasant manner,
> both in private and in public (LT 7).

This exemplary experience is ever-new on each day, lasting forever.

Entering into the mind of the servant, Julian further explains:

> Then this poor creature thinks: "Oh, how could this
> noble lord bestow more honour and joy on me than
> by showing me, who am so simple, this marvellous
> familiarity? Truly, this gives me more joy than if he
> gave me great gifts but kept a distant manner towards
> me" (LT 7).

At once, Julian reveals that the king of the example stands for the Lord Jesus, who is also our brother, and whose self-giving begets overwhelming joy:

This physical example was shown so exalted that the
human heart might be ravished and almost forget itself
for joy at this great intimacy. This is the way it is with
our Lord Jesus and us: for truly the greatest joy that
can be, as I see it, is that he who is most high and most
powerful, most noble and most worthy, is the most
lowly and most meek, the most familiar and most
courteous. ... For the most complete joy that we shall
have, as I see it, is the marvellous courtesy and
familiarity of our Father, who is our maker, in our Lord
Jesus Christ, who is our brother and our saviour (LT
7).

This beginning of a parable in Julian's text already goes far
beyond what Thomas Aquinas' example implies. Aquinas
points to the quiet, ennobling affection of highly-placed kin-
folk; Julian names the unlimited joy of a fully satisfying intimacy, blended of reverence and a love known only among
equals. The twofold dimensions of the divine encounter are
grounded in the mystery that where the enfleshed Jesus is,
there is the joy that is the sign of the Trinity.

Language serves to carry this idea and meaning through
a stylistic difference between Julian's parable and those of
the two theologians who also write parables about a king.

Anselm and Thomas take an intellective approach, specified
by an invitation to assume a set of circumstances to be true,
merely for the sake of argument. Julian leads us into an experience, with details of conversation, colour, place, and poetic
ambiguity. Julian's is closer to the parables of the Scripture,
which are also direct and narrative, and also invite multiple
levels of interpretation: for example, "A sower went out to
sow his seed" (Luke 8:6).

Further, Anselm and Thomas offer their parables once and

for all, as if the clarity of the example begets an intellectual grasp of the underlying truth. Julian ruminates over her parable, repeating and augmenting its details. The male theologians speak to the discursive intellect, with the example serving to evoke clear-cut conclusions at an abstract level. Julian comes to a deeper grasp of the mysterious truth, as she leads us with her, step-by-step, through the parable's cumulative meanings, always returning to the experience. In the end she herself enters into the meaning because the Lord gives sight to her understanding.

## Structure of Julian's Parable

*The Narrative Strategy of the Parable*: Structurally, the parable unfolds all at once, and is then repeated and intensified in parts, as Julian grows in understanding of what it means. She also gives, at the beginning, an overview of her mode of seeing this vision: she sees the lord as well as the servant, with the eye of the understanding, beholding in both a physical and a spiritual mode. Then she sees the servant spiritually, but still visibly; and she sees the lord only spiritually. These modes of vision correspond to her deepening understanding of the parable.

The central action of the story is that the servant jumps at the chance to do what the lord asks. He is so heedless of danger, so driven by love, that he falls into a ditch. He suffers most from not knowing that his lord is still near and ready to comfort him. He also suffers from pain and weakness. He is blind mentally and so numbed that he almost forgets that he ever loved. He cannot help himself rise, and there seems to be no one else to help him. Finally—and this is most strange—he lies in a large, hard, painful place. The lord, meanwhile, continues to look on him with love, and without blame: for the servant got into all this trouble in trying to carry out his lord's will.

Now there is a move to a new level of meaning: The lord looks on the servant not only as he is but also as he will be. He looks on him now as he is with compassion and pity. He looks upon him as he will be with enjoyment, taking delight in him. Then Julian calls to mind "that other showing", probably the sixth, where God appears as a lord in his own house, presiding at a great feast, and taking no position of rank among his friends. This is the destiny for all those who serve God in any degree while they are on earth.

After this interruption Julian translates into colloquial discourse the Lord's meaning in his merriment over bringing his servant to this eternal feast: "What trouble and pain my servant has suffered for my sake. Should I not repay him for this? This makes good sense; but I am all goodness. Hence, should I not pour out on him a better gift than simply restoring him to his erstwhile wholeness? Should I not give him a reward? I will not merely make good my servant's losses, but out of grace, give him much more" (LT 51). At this moment we realize that we have been listening to a story with only a beginning and an end—but with no middle. How did the servant get out of the ditch? We are not told at this point—only that he will be brought to a restful enjoying and great honour by God's grace.

But not until he has learned, from his fall into the gully, to work in human fashion. We learn this when Julian asks what work the servant labourer does. She announces that "there is a treasure in the earth which the lord loves" (LT 51), and the servant will be a gardener, digging and watering and bringing forth fruit. Then she returns to mulling over the parable from the beginning. Gradually she comprehends that the lord is indeed God, in rest and peace. The servant is the first Adam, and then Adam as standing for all who came after him, and finally Christ in union with his members: "One man is all men, and all men are one man". With the first creation, humanity is one in Adam, the man of dust and death; and with the resurrection humanity is one in Christ, in a transformed existence.

Matching the colloquial speech of the Father is one from the Son: "Lo, my dear Father, I stand before you in Adam's old garment, ready to start forth and to run. I wish to be on the earth to do you honour when it is your will to send me" (LT 51). The foundation for answering her question about blame now unfolds: that there was only a single garment shows that there is nothing between the Godhood and the manhood. The Son's will was ever kept intact. God who can never attribute blame to the Son sees us when he sees the Son, and sees us as we will be when the work of the Son is complete. The Son is the Wisdom of the Father, who shows us the Way, which is the path of longing and desire. Yet on that path humanity often stumbles and falls.

*Meaning of the Fall*: Julian returns from time to time to that crucial event in her story—Adam, helplessly trapped in the gully, where he had fallen. In fact, her understanding "was led into the Lord" at the very time she saw the servant in his fallen state (LT 52).

This prepares the way for finding in the idea of "falling" the key to the story of redemption, as it unfolded in Julian's contemplation.

In the thirteenth showing, in chapters immediately preceding the narrating of the parable, Julian has been teaching us about falling into sin and rising again. "By his sufferance we fall", then by mercy and grace we are raised to greater

107

joys (LT 35). She illustrates her point by citing the example of John Beverly: God "suffered" him to fall into sin and then bestowed on him more joys than if he had not fallen (LT 38). We are not to despair over our falling, for our falling does not block out God's love. Indeed, that very falling is a further occasion for Christ to show himself as the one who says: "I preserve and defend you and keep what I have made forever".

We fall into the mischief of sin from fickleness, frailty, and folly in ourselves, and from external forces overpowering our will, such as when we are in torment, sorrow, and woe. In any case we fall through blindness (LT 47). The mark of sin is shame (LT 48)—as if we have lost control and will lose our way, while being forced to wallow in the soil of the earth. But in this shameful state "the sweet eye of pity never turns away from us, nor does the working of mercy ever cease" (LT 48).

Moreover, grace "works" our shameful falling into a glorious rising (LT 48): we are like dough which has fallen into a shapeless mass, but which the hands of the baker "works" and re-forms so that the yeast within can transform the mass into beautiful loaves of bread.[4] If we collaborate with evil and thereby fall, not into mischief alone, but into a deliberate opposition to the Good, God's goodness makes a treaty of peace with us in our wrath and "in our contrarious falling" (LT 49).

Within the parable itself the references to the servant's shameful fall are progressively interpreted, depending on who is signified by the servant. There are three constants: the servant falls into shame and sorrow; the Lord looks on him constantly with love; and the servant's falling and woe will be turned into honour and bliss.

First, insofar as the servant is the first Adam, the Lord

takes no harder the falling of any creature that shall be saved than he took the falling of Adam (LT 53).

Second, inasmuch as the servant is all humanity, through the first Adam, the "falling" of each one is in some way in all: "We have in us the mischief of Adam's falling" (LT 52). This is the shameful side of the fall: the mischief and blindness that is in Adam and all his progeny. We are in diverse ways broken in our feeling by Adam's falling and made dark and blind (LT 52). We fall, to the extent that we are blind, and we rise again, in the degree that the eye of our understanding is opened. But inasmuch as we share also in the nature of the Christ-servant, we have in us his final uprising (LT 52).

Third, insofar as the servant is Christ, the fall is shameful and degrading, but in his fall there is no blame. The Christ-servant "fell" into the earthly condition: "the falling of the Son was the taking of our kind" (LT 51). In fact, his fall is more appropriately, at times, called something which befell him, rather than a fall: the Christ-servant did not fear what would befall him, from the time that he was fallen into the maiden's womb (LT 51).

Simultaneously while seeing the servant Julian also sees the face of God focused on him: "Unceasingly his loving Lord most tenderly beholds him" (LT 51). Julian studies the expressions on God's face, and thereby learns what the divine features reveal. As Augustine says: "God's face is the power by which he is made known to them that are worthy."[5] Also the divine face sometimes designates God's presence in the church.[6]

When God sees the servant as Adam, he looks on him with compassion and pity (LT 51). So likewise God looks on us in our solidarity with Adam. He permits us to fall in order that we may come to know our own wretchedness

(LT 61). For as the corporate Adam we are not yet ready to be the city of God in which the Lord will rule by love (LT 51).

Inasmuch as the servant is Christ, the Lord looks on him with joy and bliss, rejoicing in the Son who is equal with the Father (LT 51). The Lord also rejoices in the corporate Christ, in whom is shown both the mischief of Adam's falling and the wisdom and goodness of God (LT 52). The Lord's face shows his delight in this falling because of the rising and increased fullness of joy that will follow the fall (LT 52). "This falling and woe will be turned into high, surpassing honour and endless bliss" (LT 51).

As always, whatever Julian is taught, she teaches us in turn. As she tells us initially, where Christ is, there is the Trinity; and it is so in this showing, too: for she beholds in the falling of the servant both Christ's union with the sin and pain of humanity and also "the might, wisdom and love" which is the Trinity turning all to his honour and our joy (LT 62). The counsel she develops from this sight is systematically practical. She acknowledges that the shame of our sin could draw us into despair (LT 73). But we need not be surprised that we fall into sin, given our natural instability (LT 76). In fact, she knows of no lover of Christ who is always kept from sin (LT 82). In particular, we should not grieve over sin that befalls us against our will (LT 82).

On the other hand, we must not be careless, precipitating our own fall into sin (LT 79). We should constantly fear for ourselves, not knowing when we will fall (LT 79). The chief precaution we should take is to pray that we do not fall blindly, and if we fall, to rise quickly (LT 76). In this way we have a defence against the enemy, who relishes chiding us with our broken promises (LT 76). We should realize that the fiend loses more by our rising than he wins by our falling (LT 77).

Christ also "works" to withdraw us from sin. For as by feebleness and folly we fall, so by mercy and grace we rise again (LT 77). "If by our blindness and wretchedness we fall at any time, we rise quickly, knowing the sweet touching of grace, and purposefully amend our ways, according to the teaching of holy church..." (LT 52). There we shall find solace in the community of the faithful, in the body of Christ which is never broken (LT 61).

Christ wants us to enjoy his love, more than to sorrow over our falling (LT 81). For "in beholding God, we fall not, and in beholding self we stand not" (LT 82). He may even allow us to fall harder than we did before, so that we can learn even better the depths of his marvellous love. He loses no time in raising us up, calling to us lovingly and touching us with grace (LT 61). To draw us to him, our courteous Lord not only calls to us and touches us, but stirs up our hearts from within, deterring us from undue self-accusing and urging us to turn to him (LT 79). But if we still refuse to respond, he waits for us, alone and faithfully (LT 79). We think, of course, of the father waiting for the prodigal son.

But Julian thinks specifically of Mother Christ. Here we are invited to replace the fall that is sin with a fall that signifies trust. In our sinful condition "we are to fall onto our Lord's breast, as the child into its mother's arms" (LT 74). And the fall into sin that God permits in order to teach us our need for grace is likened to the fall the mother "suffers" for the growing child, when she allows it to endure salutary pain that also causes her pain:

The mother may "suffer" the child to fall sometimes
and be disquieted in several ways for its own profit;
but she can never "suffer" any form of peril to come

111

to the child, because of her love. And even though our earthly mother could "suffer" her child to perish, our heavenly mother Jesus cannot "suffer" us that are his children to perish: for he is all power, all wisdom, all love—and none but he is so (LT 61).

Even if we have cast ourselves into the depths of the mercy of Mother Jesus, we may still feel sorrow and fear. Yet we can be sure that Jesus is acting like a wise mother, who, pitying us all the while, "suffers" us to mourn and weep until it is the best time to embrace us with comfort (LT 61).

Thus the story of the fall, from Julian's highly integrated perspective, comes full circle.

Her mode of mystical understanding comes into play intermittently, by this "leading of her understanding" into God. and at the same time by the meaning "descending into her soul". Her contemplation is like the flowing and receding of the ocean-tide, whose rhythm is regulated by the hidden energies of the universe.

## *Endnotes*

1. Mark Jordan, in *Notes and Commentary* 6 (Fall, 1983), 5, from Thomas Aquinas, *Collationes super Credo in Deum*. Jordan's rendering is very free, but nonetheless catches the spirit of the original. See "In Symbolum Apostolorum scilicet 'Credo in Deum', expositio", *Opuscula Theologica*, II, ed., Fr. Raymundi M. Spiazzi, O.P. (Rome, Marietti, 1954) II: 202.

2. *Cur Deus Homo* in St. Anselm. *Basic Writings*, trans. S. N. Deane (La Salle, Ill., Open Court Publishing Co., 1962) 233.

3. *Cur Deus Homo* 267.

4. "'*Working*' is a key word in Julian's text running a whole gamut of shades of meaning, from labour necessary in the effort to discipline the self in spiritual life (c. 41) to a working which, like that of yeast in dough, is a transforming, rising agent: 'mercy werkyth turning to us althyng to good' (c. 48...)" "Visions and Revisions: A Further Look at the Manuscripts of Julian of Norwich," *Studies in Bibliography* 42 (1989) 114.
5. "Expositions on the Psalms", *Nicene and Ante-Nicene Fathers* 8, 44 (On Psalm 11).
6. 'Expositions on the Psalms", 198 (On Psalm 68).

# THE PARABLE OF THE LORD AND THE SERVANT

## (b) *Human Depth Experiences: God Leads Us*

The lord and king of Julian's mysterious parable is not one who rules from afar but one who leads to a kingdom in the making. This is the nature of his "royal lordship". In fact, "leading" is a core concept.

### *"Leading" in the Parable*

That God does not either coerce us, nor leave us utterly to our own devices, but gently *leads* us, even into the mystical life, is a repeated motif in the parable itself. When Julian has introduced the dilemma which has occasioned the parable—the paradox of human and divine judgment about sin— she does not allow us to slide over the fact of sin in order to enjoy the more attractive parts of the story. Instead she says at the outset: "All heavenly and all earthly things that

113

pertain to heaven are included in these two judgments. And the more understanding—by the gracious *leading* of the Holy Ghost—that we have of these two, the more we shall see and know our failings" (LT 45).

In the course of the unfolding of the parable, Julian refers repeatedly to the leading of her understanding into deep mystical prayer, where she encounters divine verities and the living God. The inward dimension of the showing, by which God's joy in salvation is disclosed, is attributed to "the *leading* of my understanding into the Lord" (LT 51). At the point where she alternates between the parable itself, and the flashback to the sixth showing (of the divine banquet), she sees these two simultaneously: "Then my understanding *was led* into the first, keeping both in mind" (LT 51). At the moment when the example vanishes, though some form of "sight" remains, she has another intense spiritual experience: "and our good Lord *led forth* my understanding in sight and showing to the end" (LT 51).

This leading is connected explicitly with the metaphor of Jesus as mother, in an experience which in part shows the very Godhead and heaven itself:

> The mother can lay the child tenderly to her breast;
> but our tender mother Jesus can intimately *lead* us into
> his blessed breast through his sweet, open side, and
> show therein, in part, the Godhead and the joys of
> heaven, with a spiritual certainty of endless bliss (LT
> 60).

This text echoes, of course, St. Paul's teaching that we see now in part (as in a mirror) and in heaven face to face (1 Cor. 13:12). Gregory of Nyssa is likewise close to Julian's language, when he says: "Moses sought to see God, and this is the instruction he received on how he is to see Him: seeing God means following Him wherever He might lead."[1]

But even with the help of this high mystical enlightenment, leading into the very heart of God, Julian admits that she is still not fully satisfied in her probing of her dilemma over the two paradoxical judgments. "But notwithstanding all this *leading forth*, the wondering over the example never left me; for I thought it had been given as an answer to my desire, and yet I could not gain from it understanding adequate to set me at ease" (LT 51).

In the same chapter she tries to explain this action of God under the conventional metaphor of touch, which (in contrast, for example, to "grasp", used of the wicked spirit) shows how gently the Lord lures her. As is usual for her, a symbolic image accompanies her insight:

> The voluminous folds of his garments, [the Lord's]
> which were fair, and flaming about him, signify that
> he has enclosed within himself all heavens and all joy
> and bliss. And this was shown in a touch, where I say:
> "My understanding *was led* into the Lord." In that I
> saw him greatly enjoying the merciful restoring that he
> will and shall bring his servant by his grace (LT 51).

This gentle, non-coercive leading is unlike Rolle's more violent image of a divine "seizing", perilously close to the "grasping" of the evil spirit.[2] He says: "O Shining Love, come into me and *seize* me with Yourself, so that I may be present before the Face of my Creator!"[3] Furthermore, Rolle's experience is personal and individual whereas Julian's relates to the restoring of all creatures to be saved.

Similarly, in her sight of the servant, Julian pierces that same divine mystery. She sees that the state to which humanity is restored is immeasurably greater than that from which it fell:

> And thus to see this surpassing ennobling my understanding *was led* into God at the same time as I saw the servant falling (LT 52).

Later, she reminds us, in a summary, how holistic her deepest experiences of God are: grounded in nature, ennobled by union with the Christ-Servant, fructified by the Spirit whom Christ has sent to lead us:

> I understood that sensuality is grounded in kind, in mercy, and in grace. It is this ground which enables us to receive gifts that *lead* to eternal life. . . . Thus, in the ground of nature, working with mercy, the Holy Ghost gently breathes into us gifts *leading* to endless life. And thus my understanding *was led* by God:
> —to see in him, and to understand
> —to perceive and to know
> that our soul is a made Trinity,
> like to the unmade blessed Trinity,
> known and loved without beginning (LT 55).

And in the same vein: "In this endless love we *are led* and kept by God and never shall be lost" (LT 53).

## Difficulties

Given this pattern by which she expresses her mystical insight—always the hardest to describe—we are now in a better position to clarify some passages which have puzzled, or perhaps misled, commentators and translators.

The first hinges on the origin of the servant, who is, in fact, the very goodness of God. Julian repeats her insight that God is present in all as goodness by the use of a slightly varied refrain:

> And yet I wondered from whence the servant came.
> For, I saw in the Lord that
> > *he has within himself endless life and all manner of*
> > *goodness*
> [All life and goodness], except for that treasure which
> is in the earth.
> > *and that was grounded in the Lord in wondrous depths*
> > *of endless love.*
> But this treasure that was in the earth did not fully
> honour the Lord until the servant had thus nobly
> prepared and brought it before the Lord
> > *in himself present*[4] (LT 51).

The final variation on the refrain affirms that when the servant brings the treasure in the earth [humanity] to fullness of life it is the same eternal life which already exists in the Servant-Christ. Hence, it is "present in himself" eternally— or, as Clifton Wolters translates the earlier lines: "And that treasure too had its being in the wonderful depths of his eternal love."[5] Such a reading is bolstered by a later passage where she affirms that "our soul is ... so deeply grounded in God and ... endlessly *treasured*" (LT 56).

Another difficulty is in a passage in which Julian reports contemplating the love with which the Father beholds the servant, not yet understood to be Christ united to humanity. Here Julian observes:

117

And thus the loving Lord beholds him [the servant] continually and most tenderly, and now with a double expression:

the first outwardly, very meekly and mildly and with great compassion and pity;

and another inwardly, more spiritual (and this was shown by a *leading* of my understanding into the Lord) which I saw him greatly enjoying: because of the worshipful resting and ennobling that he will and shall bring his servant to by his plenteous grace (LT 51).

Colledge and Walsh read this to mean that the antecedent of *which* is *my understanding* and that the Sloane text as it stands does not otherwise make sense.[6] But once we read the passage for its implicit parallelisms, it becomes intelligible. Julian is contemplating a twofold way by which the Lord beholds Christ and his members: with an expression of compassion, which can be understood in human terms, outwardly; and with an expression of joy over the final bliss to which mankind is to be led—an insight which comes with the help of a profound mystical grace, or "leading of her understanding into the Lord". It was this for which Christ prayed: "that my joy might be in you, and your joy might be complete" (John 15:11).

Julian herself says this more directly in a later passage in the same chapter: "And this was shown in a touch, where I say: 'My understanding *was led* into the lord, in which I saw him [the Father] highly *enjoying* because of the noble restoring to which he will and shall bring his servant by his plenteous grace'" (LT 51). In both cases the substance of joy is the restoring of the servant to a bliss which exceeds what has been lost (LT 51).

A third difficult passage becomes clear when considered in the light of the meaning of the whole parable—whereby the lord and servant relationship becomes one of equality. The passage reads:

> The sitting of the Father symbolizes his Godhead,
>     that is to say, showing rest and peace;
>         —for in the Godhead there is no travail.
> That he showed himself as Lord indicates our humanity.
>     The standing of the servant indicates travail.
>
> Standing at one side and on the left
> indicates that he was not worthy to stand
> directly in front of the Lord (LT 51).

That he showed himself as lord to symbolize our humanity means, as is said later, "that he made man's soul to be his own city and his dwelling place" (LT 51), the city which in his eternal purpose he had prepared for the Son (LT 51). Or, as Julian says in the same chapter: "At the time when he [the Father] of his goodness wishes to show himself to man, he shows himself familiarly, as man; nonetheless, I saw truly that we ought to understand and believe that the Father is not man" (LT 51). In the Father is all the goodness that will become the great city. The passage has been translated by some to mean that the image of the lord stands for authority or governance, and by others in such a way as to obscure the Trinitarian mystery of the interplay—inter-circling—between Father and Son.[7] This is more explicit where Julian says: "The honourable city in which our Lord Jesus sits is our sensuality, in which he is enclosed. And our natural substance is enclosed in Jesus, with the blissful soul of Christ sitting in rest in the Godhead" (LT 56). This city is established in the "highest point" or mystical Self: "I saw that God is in our sensuality. For the very point in which our soul is made sensual, in that same point is the city of God, ordained for God from the beginning" (LT 55).

This interpretation is confirmed by still another use of the metaphor of lordship. There it is implied that the Lord's creation lures us to go beyond what is visible in order to seek the lord and the heavenly city, established within the mystical Self:

> Everything that he has made shows his lordship.
> Understanding of this was bestowed at the same time
> in the example of a creature who sees great splendour
> and kingdoms belonging to a lord; and when, after
> having seen all the splendour that is beneath, then,
> marvelling, that creature was stirred to seek above to
> the high place where the lord dwells, knowing through
> reason that the lord's dwelling is in the highest place
> (LT 67).

Julian does not interpret this parable as a manifestation of God's authority; rather, it unveils a divine strategy for motivating us to seek what is best, where true happiness resides:

> And thus I understood truly that our soul can never
> have rest in things that are beneath it. And when it
> comes above all creatures into the Self, even then it
> cannot linger in the beholding of that Self. But all its
> beholding is blissfully fixed on the maker dwelling
> therein (LT 67).

Perhaps the overarching difficulty in reading Julian is to enter into the mystery that the lord becomes a servant. His

power is not exercised as a dominating authority, but as trans-
formative, empowering his creatures:

> At this point [after yielding the soul, with all mankind,
> into the Father's hands] *he began to exercise his power.*
> For he went into hell, and when he was there he raised
> up, out of the deep abyss, the great root which
> rightfully was knit to him in high heaven; ... our foul
> mortal flesh that God's Son took on himself, which was
> Adam's old garment, was made fair now—white and
> bright and of endless cleanness, wide and ample, fairer
> and richer than was the clothing which I saw before
> on the Father ... (LT 51).

We can recall here that midway in the narrative of the
lord and the servant Julian made an abrupt shift of imagery
from the focus on the garments to the image of the treasure
in the earth (LT 51). The only connection between the two
was to explain the clothing of the servant, which was that
of a labourer, and then to answer the question as to what
work he would do: he would be a gardener and by hard
labour bring out of the earth treasures of food and drink
to please the lord. Here there is a similar abrupt shift but
in the opposite sequence: the servant is seeking out the old
root of humanity in the depths of the earth; and when he
has done so, the splendid garments he wears signify his victory
and triumph. In this passage we first see the work the servant
is doing, and then we see how appropriate his garments are
to the gloriously fulfilled task. The Christ-servant was knit
by kinship to the great root—mankind sprung from Adam.
The old garment that is our flesh he transforms into a beauty
greater than that of the clothing seen on the Father.[8]

Into such mysteries Julian's understanding is led, by the
pathways of images.

## Endnotes

1. *Commentary on the Song of Songs* VI (888A), quoted by Andrew Louth, *The Origins of the Christian Mystical Tradition* (Oxford, Clarendon Press, 1981) 88–89.

2. See, for example, LT 66, where, speaking of the fiend, Julian says: "with his paws he held me by the throat and would have strangled me."

3. Richard Rolle, *The Mending of Life*, in *The Fire of Love and The Mending of Life*, trans. M.L. del Mastro (New York, Doubleday & Co., Inc., 1982) 84.

4. Colledge and Walsh say (II, 532, l. 208): "*in hym selfe present* ... If this is not a scribal error ... one may question whether it is not a bungled version of 'in his self presence.'" Clifton Wolters also had difficulty with this phrase, rendering it: "But its worth to him depended on the servant's careful preparation of it, *and his setting it before him personally.*" (p. 147).

5. Wolters 147.

6. "It is noteworthy that the usually intelligent and perceptive SS scribes do not make sense of this difficult passage." Colledge and Walsh, *A Book of Showings* II, 517, note to l. 42

7. *Revelations of Divine Love*, trans. Grace Warrack, 12th ed. (London: Methuen and Co., Ltd., 1945) 119: "And that He shewed Himself as *Lord*, betokeneth His [governance] to our manhood."
   *Revelations of Divine Love*, trans. Clifton Wolters (Baltimore, Md., Penguin Books, 1973) 149: "That he showed himself *lord* is a sign of his authority over our humanity."

8. Julian's image of the garments recalls in a general way the theory of the "garment of skin" in Gregory of Nyssa. "What is implied ... in the garment of skin is not, as Origen thought, the body as such; for in Gregory's view both the soul and the body were part of human nature in the beginning. Rather, it comprises all that implies mortality and corruptibility; and man's true nature is to enjoy the incorruptibility of the risen body." Jean Daniélou, S.J., Introduction, *From Glory to Glory Texts from*

*Gregory of Nyssa's Mystical Writings*, trans. Herbert Musurillo, S.J. (Crestwood, N.Y., St. Vladimir's Seminary Press, 1979) 11.

# THE PARABLE OF THE LORD AND THE SERVANT

## (c) *Weavings of Imagery*

Julian's recurrent theme of the leading of her understanding into God interlocks with her perception of images: "My understanding was led into God at the same time as I saw the servant falling" (LT 52). In this regard she departs from the tradition which holds that mental images are useful only as a concession to beginners, the weak—and women. She differs sharply, for example, from William of St. Thierry (ca. 1085–1148). In the widely-circulated *Golden Epistle* he urges even the novice "to keep as far away as he can from material objects or their representations" when thinking of God.[1] On the other hand, Julian is in line with that body of feminine spirituality which legitimizes the place of both body and image in prayer.[2]

Two of the most important images of the parable are that of clothing and that of the root. These in turn are related to the metaphorical references to the wilderness, the garden, and the city. The passage typifies Julian's method of blending images to suggest an underlying truth. A boss in the Norwich cathedral offers a similar interweaving of images. It shows Christ crucified to the living vine, sprung from the earth, and heavy with grapes from which the wine which is Christ's blood can burst forth. The implied scriptural text is: "I am the vine, you are the branches", (John 15:5), superimposed on the narratives of the passion and of the Eucharist.

123

In Julian's parable the imagery of clothing is the most pervasive. Each time she reviews the colour, shape, and cut of
the garments of the lord and the servant she understands
more about what they signify. In particular, she dwells on
the garment of mixed colours which is the most beautiful
of all, signifying the greater splendour that fills the heavens
when humanity is interwoven with the divine in Christ's
mystical body.

The wilderness is the place where the lord sits, awaiting
what the servant will do. The wilderness is first hinted at
in the last of the seven great pains, seen early as afflicting
the servant. These pains are simultaneously, though in different ways, the sufferings of Adam, of the individual Christ,
and of the Christ-servant.

Julian enumerates these pains as seen in a bodily vision:
the first three are pains of the body; the fourth is of the
mind; the last three are of the spirit. In the last the servant
suffers seeming abandonment, like Christ calling out to his
Father. And the servant realizes that he is not only lying
helpless and bound to his own space on the cross, but he
is bound also to the whole earth, to that wilderness where
the Lord waits. "From the time that he fell into the maiden's
womb, till his body was slain and dead, yielding then the
soul into the Father's hands with all mankind for whom
he was sent" (LT 51).

In Luke 12:22 Christ is identified with the suffering servant
of Isaiah 42, who is likewise greatly loved, and sent on a
difficult mission:

> Here is my servant whom I uphold,
>    my chosen one with whom I am pleased,
> Upon whom I have put my spirit;
>    he shall bring forth justice to the nations. (Is. 42:1)

Throughout the parable the servant bears some likeness to the suffering servant, as further described in Isaiah 40–52. In those chapters the servant undergoes change in the pursuit of a divine mission: from interior crisis, through persecution, through suffering, humiliation, and death, and finally to a triumph and elevation, with a clear message that the trials have not prevailed over his mission.[3] Similarly, in Julian, the servant undergoes a spiritual crisis: ("He had almost forgotten his own love" [LT 51]: from persecution, through suffering, humiliation and death; and finally triumph.

Specific texts in these chapters on the prophetic servant support Julian's imagery: For example, "You are my servant, he said to me/Israel, through whom I show my glory" (Is. 49:3). The wilderness where the lord was waiting was "on the earth, barren and a desert", and the lord was "alone in the wilderness". Already the desert had a potential for further revelation, for "within him was a high citadel, long and wide, full of endless heavens" (LT 51).

In this connection we can recall Isaiah 43:19: "See, I am doing something new!/Now it springs forth, do you not perceive it?/ In the desert I make a way,/in the wasteland, rivers." The wilderness where the lord waits is transformed by the divine gardener, who cultivates it and waters the growth in the proper time. There is in the earth where the gardener labours a hidden treasure, eternal life. The garden, in fact, has numerous scriptural echoes, not the least of which is that of the mustard seed, which gives birth to the kingdom of God:

> Then he said, "What is the kingdom of God like? To
> what can I compare it? It is like a mustard seed that
> a person took and planted in the garden. When it was
> fully grown, it became a large bush and the birds of

the sky dwelt in its branches. (Luke 13:18–19).

Finally, the wilderness gives way to a city so that it is said:

> The lord no longer sits on earth in the wilderness, but
> he sits on his noblest throne made most to his liking
> (LT 51).

This transformation contrasts with what Meister Eckhart does with the image of the desert, which is a ceasing of activity:

> In this way the soul enters into the unity of the Holy
> Trinity, but it may become even more blessed by going
> further, *to the barren Godhead*, of which the Trinity
> is a revelation. In this barren Godhead *activity has
> ceased* and therefore the soul will be most perfect
> when it is thrown into *the desert* of the Godhead,
> where both activity and *forms are no more* so that it
> is sunk and lost in this desert where identity is
> destroyed.[4]

For Julian the emphasis is not on the silent Godhead but on the divine activity, actual and potential. For example, in some ways God is still in the waterless desert, for Christ "is with us in heaven, true man in his own person, drawing us upward", as was shown in the spiritual thirst—the desire of Christ to have us with him (LS 52).

In summary, these four images—the wilderness, the gardener, the treasure and the city—form a web of meaning. The wilderness where the Father sits in longing, with a heavenly place of refuge within, is the undeveloped earth, fallen humanity. The treasure is a seed hidden in a field, the nucleus of the kingdom of God. Others have spoken in similar vein of the ground of being, of the mystical self, and of the reality of the divine presence within. The gardener is not only Christ—but the whole Christ—who will bring the city of God into being, with a throne on which the Father will sit. Christ, crowned with the laurels of redeemed humanity, will share equally in the Father's joys.

There are mystical texts in Scripture which illuminate this web of imagery. In Hosea, for example, it is said: "So I will allure her;/ I will lead her into the desert/and speak to her heart" (Hosea 2:16).

Other texts, especially from Isaiah, are also in harmony with the imagery of Julian's parable:

> "I am the LORD, your Holy One,/the creator of Israel, your King ..." (Is. 43:15) ... "For I put water in the desert/and rivers in the wasteland/for my chosen people to drink" (Is. 43:20) ... "Yes, the LORD shall comfort Zion ... / Her deserts he shall make like Eden,/her wasteland like the garden of the LORD;/Joy and gladness shall be found in her,/thanksgiving and the sound of song." (Is. 51:3)

As in Julian there are minglings of the imagery of the imperial role of the Lord, the hidden treasure, and the city to be built:

> "In the LORD shall be the vindication and the glory/of all the descendants of Israel" (Is. 45:25) ... "It was I who stirred up one for the triumph of justice;/ all his ways I make level/He shall rebuild my city' (Is. 45:13). ... "I will give you treasure out of the darkness,/ and riches that have been hidden away" (Is. 45:3).

The image of Christ the gardener has been used also in a widely-circulated text, contemporary with Julian. But its impact is more moralizing than mystical, and the author lacks the skill to intertwine the primary image with related images, and hence does not achieve Julian's depth or scope:

> Our Lord God is also like a gardener, for a gardener sometimes allows wicked weeds to grow in his garden, and when, through the moisture of rain, the earth grows tender, he pulls out the weeds, both root and stem. So likewise does our Lord Jesus Christ. He sometimes allows in his garden, which is man's soul, wicked deeds of sin to grow, but when the heart of man grows tender by meekness and the moisture of contrition, he then pulls out all the sins, both root and stem, and plants and arranges the herbs and fruits of good virtues in his garden and waters them with the dew of his blessed goodness, by which the soul of man shall come to everlasting joy and bliss.[5]

Illumined by a reflective reading of the text of Julian's parable, the image of the servant seems clear. It has ample scriptural basis, especially in Isaiah 40–55. It has much of the ambiguity and shifting meaning which is attributed by a recent commentator to the servant passages in Isaiah:

> These chapters 41–48 allow us to appreciate Second Isaiah's rich concept of "servant," one that continues through his writings into those of Third Isaiah. In a *positive* way the servant is God's beloved one, either all Israel (41, 8–9; 43,10; 44,11) or the prophet and his disciples (42,1; 49,3,6). Even the foreigner Cyrus (44,28) is included among God's beloved servants. In a *negative* way the servant is either Israel, blind, deaf, and robbed of dignity (42,19), guilty and sinful (43,23), or surprisingly God, for in 43, 12 servant language is used

with reference to God, burdened and weary with
Israel's sins (43,24).[6]

But why, we may yet ask, did Julian suppress the image
of kingship for so long—for fifteen years or more? Was it
only because she feared to lay bare her uneasiness about the
final benevolence of God regarding sin? Or was it because
she feared to sound heretical—as indeed she did to some
readers of later time—regarding the absence of wrath in God?

Perhaps so. But it is intriguing to note that it is precisely
the image of king (and even of bishop) that she avoids in
the short text. This is apparent when we compare from the
long text the final reference to the teaching of the parable
(LT 67) with the corresponding section in the short text (ST
22). He whom she calls in the first rendition simply "highest
lord", in the long text is named "highest bishop, most
honourable king, most noble lord". These acclamations are
reinforced by the short example of one who sees a lord's
glorious kingdom and is moved to seek out where the lord
himself dwells. The concept of lordship here is central. The
long text passage serves as a recapping of the great parable
and its final portrait of the king, again under the image of
one who presides in his city:

> And then our Lord opened my spiritual eye and showed
> me my soul in the midst of my heart. I saw my soul
> as large as if it were an endless world and as if it were
> a blissful kingdom; and by the conditions that I saw
> therein, I understood that it is a noble city. In the midst
> of that city sits our lord Jesus, God and man, a fair
> person, of large stature, highest bishop, most solemn
> king, noblest lord; and I saw him clad majestically and
> nobly. He sits in the soul . . . in peace and in rest. And
> the Godhead rules and cares for heaven and earth and

all that is—sovereign might, sovereign wisdom,
sovereign goodness. (LT 67).

In this naming of the persons in the Godhead, as power, wisdom, and goodness, Julian is in the tradition of Thomas Aquinas, who is in turn in harmony with Augustine. Aquinas places governance by appropriation in the goodness of the Holy Ghost: "To the Father is appropriated *power*, which is especially shown in creation. To the Son is appropriated *wisdom*, through which an intellectual agent acts; and therefore it is said: *Through whom all things were made*. To the Holy Ghost is appropriated *goodness*, to which belong both governance, which brings things to their proper end, and the giving of life ...."[7] But Julian (though she identifies the Lord as the Father) places governance in the Godhead, not in the Holy Ghost as an appropriation.

This is true even in the earlier text where she says:

The manhood with the Godhead sits in rest, and the
Godhead rules and governs without any instruments or
activity; and my soul is blissfully occupied with the
Godhead that is sovereign might, sovereign wisdom,
and sovereign goodness (ST 22).

In the Long Text she directly adverts to Christ as lord, prolonging her vision of him by using the imagery of clothing: "I saw him in garments of splendour" (LT 67). She touches again on the imagery of the parable when she says: "Everything he has made reveals his lordship" (LT 67). This is akin to the imagery of the psalmist, who says:

You *have crowned* the year with your bounty ...
and rejoicing *clothes* the hills.

130

The fields are *garmented* with flocks
and the valleys *blanketed* with grain.
They shout and sing for joy! (Ps. 65:12–14).

The *Showings* had begun with the crowning of thorns, a mockery of one who claimed to be a king. The chapter which recounts the lord and servant parable ends with a reversal and consummation of that crowning: we who caused the bloody, painful crowning are in the end his garland of glory: "He stands before the Father ... with a crown of precious riches on his head; for it was shown that we are his crown, a crown which is the joy of the Father, the honour of the Son, and the delight of the Holy Ghost..." (LT 51).

What is striking—perhaps revolutionary—in Julian's lord and servant parable is solidly based in scripture. The lord is king indeed. But the mutual indwelling of the Trinity manifests itself in a sharing of kingship: the Son becomes a king on earth. The Christ-king shows power, after the resurrection, after the "yielding" of the fruits of his arduous tilling of the earth. Dwelling in the soul of humanity the lord/king exercises his authority as a loving host, celebrating the union of his friends at a festive table.

By the lordship of the Holy Ghost, and by oneness with Christ, humanity shares in the metaphors of lordship: the "fair creation"—humanity restored and transformed—is not only the crown of the Christ king, but also the spouse of the Christ-king. However, the lord and king metaphors are only secondarily about power and authority. The authority is only used to send the Son to restore and transform the earth, to build a path in the wilderness, to bring forth food and make the streams flow in the desert. The power is used to break the chains of hell and bring humanity to heaven.

In some ways the parable is imbedded in the kenosis hymn

131

of Philippians 2:6-11. This hymn celebrates the Christ who was always God coming as a servant in human likeness, human in appearance. Because he became obedient even unto death on the cross, God gave him a name above all others. Hence, all are called to confess that Jesus Christ is Lord, to the glory of God the Father. And all are called to complete the kingdom of love, by everyone looking out for the interests of others as though they were one's own.

The parable is mostly about joy—the joy that follows the labour of the Christ-mother; it is about en-joyment: that is, a flowing through and returning of love, so that one can scarcely distinguish the Giver from the Gift.

Christ, the last Adam, is the risen Christ, in his corporate body: "You have ... crowned him with glory and honour./ You have given him rule over the works of your hands,/ putting all things under his feet" (Ps. 8:6-7). The risen Christ is the one into whose image all the children of God will be transformed.

The story is one of a transforming of relationship. It begins with God as Lord—that is, as creator and as providence. The proper relationship to such a Lord is as servant, totally dependent, and dedicated to doing his will in all things. The servant in the parable plays that dependent role. Then there is a shift in relationship—to that of father and son: the Son yields his soul to the Father, and at that moment begins to show his power. This power is first manifest in his descent into the "deep deepness" to the "old root" of mankind, which was properly "knit" to him in the beginning. The way is opened for a deeper relationship—that of oneness, which will take the form of the image of the vine and the branches.

Then there is no more mention of the lord and the servant relationship. Christ is now "lord", but in a lordship of mutuality and love. Appropriately, the parable is immediately followed by the affirming that God rejoices to be father and mother—for we are his children. And Christ rejoices that we are his family, as is a spouse or a wife; and he is our brother. The multiplying of these family relationships cuts away any suggestion of dominance and highlights mutuality in the transformed state of the servant. Of such is the kingdom of God.

Nor is the image of the lord one of domination but rather of compassion, and also of the nobility to which we will be raised: "And in the Lord was shown compassion and pity for Adam's woe; and in the Lord was shown the high nobility and the endless honour that mankind is come to in virtue of the passion and death of his dearworthy Son" (LT 52).

And since Christ is the one who saved us, this introduces the relationship of friend (LT 52). Christ is indeed "supreme", but specifically as "our highest, sovereign friend" (LT 76). The highest wisdom on our part is to follow the "will and counsel" of this supreme friend. His will directs our freedom, while respecting it: Whether we be in sin or free of it, his will is that we be one in his loving (LT 76). The power of the enemy is locked in his hand, and this is salutary. It corrects what is evil and fosters what is good (LT 65). For the fiend has great envy of this familiar relationship. It is his desire to make us turn away to thoughts of our weakness, cowering before a threatening monarch. He would above all have us cease taking in with joy the goodness of God—God in our midst, revealing himself as "our everlasting friend" (LT 76).

But the reflections which immediately engage Julian at the close of the parable are those on Christ as Mother. In that image she contemplates the goodness of God and the Wisdom which turns evil into a greater good than that which was lost.

133

## Endnotes

1. *The Golden Epistle*, trans. Theodore Berkeley. *The Works of William of St. Thierry 4* (Kalamazoo, Cistercian Publications, 1980) 69. A fundamental difference like this one brings doubt on the arguments of Colledge and Walsh that Julian's thought often approximates that of William (*Showings*, I, II passim).

2. See Jeffrey F. Hamburger, "A *Liber Precum* in Sélestat and the Development of the Illustrated Prayerbook in Germany", *Art Bulletin* 73 (June, 1991) 209–236, esp. 233–34.

3. See B. Renaud, "La Mission du Serviteur en Is. 42, 1–4", *Revue de las Sciences Religieuses*, 64th yr., no. 2 (Avril, 1990), 101–113. This summary is taken from p. 113.

4. W.T. Stace, *Mysticism and Philosophy* (London and Basingstoke: Macmillan, 1960) 98. The significance of Eckhart's image, and its relation to his teaching on "union without distinction", is developed in Stace's chapter on "The Problem of the Universal Core", 41–133.

5. *The Remedy Against the Troubles of Temptations*, trans. Robert Boenig, typescript 114.

6. Carroll Stuhlmueller, "The Major Prophets, Baruch, and Lamentations", in *The Catholic Study Bible*, ed. Donald Senior et al (New York and Oxford, Oxford University Press, 1990) RG 295.

7. *Summa Theologica* I.I, ques. 45, art. 6, ad. 2.

# GOD AS MOTHER

The link between the image of Christ as servant and Christ as mother is made explicit in the text shortly after the exposition of the great parable. The servant who fell into the maiden's womb, who wore the garment of our flesh, is sovereign Wisdom, whose motive in becoming human was "to carry out the service and the office of motherhood in all things" (LT 60). Wolters' translation here, though almost a paraphrase, captures admirably the spirit of this connection:

> Our Mother by nature and grace—for he would become our mother in everything—laid the foundations of his work in the Virgin's womb with great and gentle condescension. (This was shown in the first revelation when I received a mental picture of the Virgin's genuine simplicity at the time she conceived). In other words, it was in this lowly place that God most high, the supreme wisdom of all, adorned and arrayed himself with our poor flesh, ready to function and to serve as Mother in all things.[1]

God leaves an image of Wisdom in the soul of Mary, his mother, who is a mirror of wisdom and truth (LT 4). She also mirrors Christ's servanthood, she who calls herself handmaid and mother (LT 4). The three showings of Mary parallel the roles of Jesus as Mother: her conception of the Saviour makes possible his becoming our mother by kinship; her sorrowing at the cross highlights the motherhood of grace which Jesus carried out by his suffering; and her glorified state is the fulfilment of the motherhood of the Spirit which is Jesus' legacy to us as divine wisdom.

In her exploiting of the motherhood image, Julian (1) joins a biblical and patristic tradition on that theme; (2) develops it as an integral part of her text; and (3) leaves a legacy of particular richness in our effort today to find new metaphors for God.

## The Forerunners

Julian's references to Christ as Mother Wisdom have a foundation in the Book of Wisdom, where Wisdom is a female figure.

Solomon says of her:

> ... all good things together came to me in her
> company,/and countless richess at her hands;/ And I
> rejoiced in them all, because Wisdom is their leader,/
> though I had not known that she is the mother of these
> (Wisdom 7:11–12).

Other texts in the same book are easily applied to Christ:

> For she is the refulgence of eternal light,/the spotless
> mirror of the power of God,/the image of his
> goodness./And she, who is one, can do all things,/and
> renews everything while herself perduring;/And passing
> into holy souls from age to age,/she produces friends
> of God and prophets (Wisdom 7:6-7).

And in another Wisdom book it is said: "... he who is prac-
ticed in the law will come to wisdom./Motherlike she will
meet him." (Sirach 15:1-2).

Interpretations in our day note that in Jewish-Hellenistic
speculation Wisdom or the heavenly Sophia was identified
with Jesus:

> Jesus was first thought of as the final emissary of
> Wisdom, and then later identified with Wisdom itself,
> insofar as the relationship between son and father is
> expressed in terms of the relationship between the
> heavenly Sophia and God.[2]

Elizabeth Schüssler Fiorenza points out the identification of
Jesus with Sophia under the metaphor of the hen:

136

In a moving passage [Luke 13:34] Sophia laments the murder of her envoys, her prophets, who are sent in every generation to proclaim the gracious goodness and justice of God to the people of Israel.... This saying likens the ministry of Sophia-Jesus to that of a hen gathering her very own brood under her wings. But the gentleness and care of Sophia is rejected.[3]

This tradition of Christ as wisdom was transmitted by Thomas Aquinas, among others. He says that Wisdom was attributed to the Son "through Whom all things were made". For "the ordering of things is reduced to *wisdom*, and the justification of the sinner to *mercy* and *goodness* poured out superabundantly".[4]

In Isaiah the portrait of the suffering servant and the metaphor of God as mother occur in the same chapter. This text in Isaiah, from the suffering servant chapters, is one of the forerunners of a long tradition on the motherhood of God:

But Zion said, "The LORD has forsaken me;/my Lord has forgotten me,/ Can a mother forget her infant,/be without tenderness for the child of her womb?/Even should she forget,/I will never forget you." (Isaiah 49:14–15).[5]

## Julian's Appropriation of the Metaphor

Julian's motherhood metaphor has as its primary purpose to reveal the intimacy which God in the Trinity establishes with creatures, and secondarily to portray the closeness of Christ to humanity. The metaphor does not depend for its force on stereotypes of motherhood.

*What is Motherhood?* Some basic stereotypes found in spiritual writers beginning with Anselm are that the mother is generative, sacrificial in giving birth, loving and tender, and nurturing.[6] Julian's text, especially with reference to the motherhood of Christ in the Eucharist, does indeed reflect these maternal functions. This has led some to conclude that Julian is merely portraying Mother Christ as nourishing the faithful in the sacraments of Baptism and the Eucharist, symbolized by the water and blood which flow from his side as milk from the mother's breast. But even here, the symbolism is fundamentally mystical. There is a long tradition portraying the open heart of Christ as the fountain of wisdom:

> According to Rahner, the mystical as opposed to the strictly sacramental interpretation of the side-wound has its principal source in the writings of Origen ... "the mystically favored man of the spirit drinks the living water of wisdom."[7]

As summarized by Jeffrey Hamburger, this symbolism, mainly transmitted through Augustine, centres on the verse in the Song of Songs (8:1): "Oh, that you were my brother,/ nursed at my mother's breasts!" The evangelist John, as an archetypal contemplative, mystic and visionary, is repeatedly portrayed not only as one drinking, but as a suckling at the breast of Christ. This concept appears in both paraliturgical prayerbooks and mystical handbooks, as well as in the liturgy itself, especially in the Office for the Feast of John the Evangelist.[8]

In a miniature described in *The Rothschild Canticles*, Hamburger points out "a striking symmetry to the gestures of Christ and Wisdom, as if to express their identity".[9]

But already Julian has implicitly defined "fatherhood" in almost the same way as motherhood: as the source of being, as love, as foreseeing wisdom—realized through the second person:

> Our high Father, God Almighty, who is being, knew
> us and loved us before all time; in this knowing, and
> in his marvelous deep charity, by the foreseeing council
> of all the blessed Trinity, he willed that the second
> person of the blessed Trinity should become our
> mother ... (LT 59).

*God is Mother*: In what sense, then, is God not only a parent but specifically a mother? In another context, Julian sets forth the "proper" meaning of motherhood in its divine timelessness. These are the motherhood of *kind*—that is, (1) the bond according to nature, that makes the mother the closest of kin to the child; (2) the motherhood of *love*, that flows naturally from this kinship; and (3) the motherhood of *wisdom and knowing*, that puts good in the place of evil and guides our lives towards the purpose for which we are ordained (LT 60).

For purposes of contemplating this mystery, Julian applies "motherhood" to the persons of the Trinity, each in turn, all the while stressing the indivisibility of the Trinity. For these properties flow in and out of each other in the mutuality of the one love:

I understand three ways of beholding motherhood in God:

> The first is grounded in our being created;
> The second is the assuming of our nature—
>     and there begins the motherhood of grace;
> And the third is the motherhood of deeds—
>     and therein is a pouring out, by
>     that same grace, of length and
>     height and depth without end.
> And all is one love (LT 59).

Even more explicitly, she reasons that motherhood is the attribute appropriated to the second person, because in this motherhood lies the answer to the question explored in the lord and servant parable: why God does not see us as "blameworthy" for our sin. Her answer has been, of course, that God sees us in our union with Christ, specifically in the "godly will" by which we never cease to will the good. It is because the motherhood of Jesus is central to the understanding of this teaching that motherhood centres on Christ as Wisdom and as Jesus—one person—doubly united to those who are to be saved.

*Jesus as Mother*: In defining Jesus as mother, Julian's metaphor builds on the bond between mother and child rather than on the differences between male and female:

> Thus Jesus Christ who does good against evil is our true mother. We have our being of him in whom the ground of motherhood takes its origin, with all the sweet loving protection that eternally follows. As truly as God is our father, just as truly God is our mother; and that he showed in all, and especially in those sweet words where he says: "I am: that is to say: I am: the power and goodness of the fatherhood; *the wisdom of the motherhood*; I am: the light and grace that is all blessed love (LT 59).

Hence, Jesus is truly our mother by nature, in virtue of our first creation; and he is our true mother by grace, by taking our created nature. All the lovely deeds and all the sweet natural services of motherhood are the properties of the second person. For in him we have the godly will whole and safe without end, in nature and in grace, of the goodness proper to him (LT 59).

In attributing motherhood to God Julian elevates the bond of love which unites parents and children. She acknowledges the debt that is owed to fathers and mothers—by God's command:

> And in this I saw that all our debt that we owe, by God's command, to fatherhood and motherhood, because of God's fatherhood and motherhood, is fulfilled in true loving of God. This the blessed love of Christ accomplishes in us. And this was shown throughout, and especially in the high, abundant words where he says: "I am the one whom you love" (LT 61).

This position contrasts sharply with that of Walter Hilton, who divides love—as he does prayer—between earthly and spiritual, even with regard to natural ties:

> ... the carnal love of father and mother, and of other friends in the world, does not weigh upon him [the lover of Jesus]: it is cut right out of his heart with the sword of spiritual love, so that he has no more affection toward father, mother or any secular friend than he has for another person, unless he sees or feels in them more grace or more virtue than in other people, except for this: he would rather that his father and mother had the same grace that some other people have, but nevertheless if they are not like that, then he loves others better than them; and that is charity.[10]

Whenever we love rightly, it is Christ loving within us.

*Julian's Uniqueness:* Sometimes in other authors the femininity of God is used to support a notion that in God there is both wrath and tenderness, with motherhood standing for God's tenderness. Such is the teaching of the *Ancrene Riwle*, which (on the authority of St. Anselm) offers a picture of a tender mother-Jesus fending off the threatening arm of the wrathful Father:

> He [Jesus] put Himself between us and His Father who
> was threatening to strike us, as a mother full of pity
> puts herself between the stern angry father who is going
> to strike it.[11]

This picture is directly contrary to Julian's portrayal of a God in whom there is no wrath. Anselm's words reveal his teaching on the harsh justice of God. Hence, similarities between Julian's motherhood metaphor and Anselm's are only superficial. Nonetheless, commentators have unduly fastened on Anselm's writings as significant in understanding Julian. For example, Grace Jantzen speaks of Anselm as one "to whose teaching Julian's often bears resemblance...."[12] And also: "It is worth quoting Anselm at some length because, as we can see, many of his thoughts are close to those of Julian."[13]

In support of this position, Jantzen quotes Anselm as saying: "If you [Christ as mother] had not died you would not have brought forth."[14] But Julian does not say this. Rather, she is closer to Wisdom theology, which, as Schüssler-Fiorenza explains, teaches that:

> The Sophia-God of Jesus does not need atonement or
> sacrifices. Jesus' death is not willed by God but is the
> result of his all-inclusive praxis as Sophia's prophet.[15]

And furthermore:

> Jesus' execution, like John's, results from his mission

142

and commitment as prophet and emissary of the Sophia-
God who holds open a future for the poor and outcast
and offers God's gracious goodness to all the children
of Israel without exception. . . .

The suffering and death of Jesus, like that of John and
all the other prophets sent to Israel before him, are not
required in order to atone for the sins of the people
in the face of an absolute God, but are the result of
the violence against the envoys of Sophia [Wisdom]
who proclaim God's unlimited goodness and the
equality and election of *all* her children in Israel.[16]

For Julian, unlike Anselm, the motive of the Incarnation
is not the necessity of atoning for sin. Rather, it is the desire
of Christ "to become our mother in all things", including
those which divine creativity could only accomplish in
created beings.

## Contemporary Overtones:
### God As Mother in Today's Spirituality

Notwithstanding its roots in the Wisdom tradition, there
is still today a reluctance among some to thinking of God—
and especially Jesus—under the image of mother. This reluctance seems to spring from the persistence of old stereotypes
about women—as the source of evil, as by nature inferior
to man, as created primarily to be the servant of man, and
as lacking in the fullness of human reason. It is this image
of woman that makes it difficult for some to find in God
any feminine likeness. But the motherly image is a corrective
against the notion which has long prevailed that God is

actually male, and, in consequence, the male is to exercise the part of God over women.

Scholars have not been in agreement in placing Christ as central to the motherhood of God tradition as Julian does. If the feminine image of God cannot be rejected, then it is easier, in a framework of anti-feminism, to connect that image with the Holy Spirit, who is hidden, who did not appear historically, and who manifests love. For example, in assessing that tradition and in speculating on the direction it will take, Yves Congar contends that "Ultimately Christian reflection will come down on the side of expressing God's femininity chiefly by and in the Spirit."[17] Congar's conjecture is built on the stereotype of the woman as carrying out the work initiated by another, as the Spirit was sent by Christ. But quite the reverse from what is in Congar's conjecture, in Julian's text the weakest attribution of divine motherhood metaphor is to the Holy Spirit. Julian touches only in passing on the Holy Spirit as feminine, while she puts in the forefront the teaching that Jesus is our mother: in our eternal birth, in our birth in time, and in our re-birth into life everlasting. She thus firmly associates Jesus as mother with the Trinity as mother.

By rooting her motherhood symbolism in Mother Wisdom, Julian transcends the gender stereotypes that divide men and women into masculine and feminine. As we have seen, she thus avoids portraying God as simply "a motherly father", who adds to maleness the tenderness and approachableness of the mother. Mary, the mother of Jesus, is seen as mirroring divine wisdom, not as a feminine figure softening the heart of a Christ-judge or the harshness of a divine warrior. Hence, God really is Mother Wisdom, for a woman on this earth reflects that wisdom in visible form.

A persistent objection against naming God as mother arises

from the biblical tradition in which Jesus addresses God as father, and never as mother. A contemporary scholar deals as follows with this difficulty. He notes that from creation and providence there arises a relationship known as "Lord", not as parent. This is in harmony with the thrust of Julian's parable:

> The ambiguity of the Father concept is removed when a clear distinction is made between the *creation of the world* and the *begetting of the son*. From the act of creation a father-relationship strictly so-called does not arise between God and his creatures. *From creation and providence God is known only as "Lord".*[18]

It is in relation to the Son that God can be known as Father. This title might just as well be "Mother", for it indicates—not authority—but the indissoluble bonds of familial relationship between humanity and God because Christ took on our humanity:

> It is only in his relationship with his Son that God can literally be called "Father" [more properly Mother]. Therefore belief in God the Father starts from recognition of the Son, not from God's omnipotence and creation. As Father of the Son, God creates heaven and earth. Through the doctrine of the Trinity God's name "Father" is indissolubly linked to Jesus the Son. The doctrine of the Trinity does not deify Christ but "christifies" God, because it pulls the Father into the life-story of the Son.[19]

Julian makes central to the mother image the birthing function of the mother, to signify the new humanity that is to come. Furthermore, motherhood exists in God as an archetype, in its fullness, and not as a limiting set of functions. That is, it is not that God is like a mother, but mothers make visible a function and relationship that is first and foremost in God.

Thus, Julian not only avoids the stereotypes but reverses them, while leaving intact the male-female distinction. Gender stereotypes were based on domination—of male over female. Domination does not figure in Julian's vision: God is inseparably courteous—worthy of reverence—and familiar, and all even-Christians are to be bonded in love. The medieval stereotype identified woman with the origin and transmission of evil, beginning with Eve. Not only does Julian not mention Eve, but she sees Wisdom as transforming evil into good.

Another aspect of the female stereotype held that woman could not be trusted. But trustworthiness is the heart of what "mother" means in Julian's concept. This is how Jessica Powers, a poet of mysticism, translates that concept, as she found it in Julian's book.

The poem is called "Millet's 'Feeding Her Birds'":

> Millet the artist has provided me
> with all I ask for in biography.
>
> These children and the mother and a bowl—
> here is the scene which circumscribes my soul.
>
> Fledglings of peace whose need is their defense—
> these are my insights into innocence.
>
> I would be one of them; if wish be heard,
> this round one leaning forward like a bird,
>
> her hands behind her and her lifted face
> waiting its mouthful. Let my day erase

its wary woe for what she knows of trust,
which is the purest homage of our dust.

Her peasant childhood motivates my will
to take my given portion and be still;

or if there must be words, to speak none other
than: O my Mother God, my God and Mother.

(1984) ("The image of God as Mother comes from
Julian of Norwich."—Jessica Powers)[20]

There is one final, and very powerful, objection to the
feminine naming of God—not to its practice but to its power
to transcend female stereotypes. After reviewing some of
Julian's feminine metaphors for God, Rosemary Ruether concludes:

But since both the human and divine person of Christ
was firmly established in mediaeval thought as male,
this means that mothering or female qualities are taken
into the male. In Christ the male gains a mode of
androgyny, of personhood that is both commanding
and nurturing. But it is doubtful that Julian's society
would have allowed her to reverse the relation and give
to women, through Christ, the right to exercise male
prerogatives.[21]

Faced with this objection we can recall again that it is the
title "Lord" which designates power and authority in God.
There is nothing universal in assimilating the Hebrew patriarchal metaphor to the parent image. Furthermore, Julian sees

in her Mother-Christ not only female functions, such as birthing, and female stereotypes, such as tenderness, but also, as we saw above, steadfastness, which was often denied of women in the Middle Ages. It is precisely as "mother" that Christ has this quality of trustworthiness, not as a trait coming from his maleness. Hence, the very image of woman that is attributed to Christ is already revised from its medieval forerunners.

Secondly, Julian herself assumes both male and female prerogatives in repeatedly telling us that she is a stand-in for her even-Christians, male and female. She does not take on the stereotyped role of "spiritual mother", but without qualification speaks of her experience and her way as unrelated to gender. Thus in herself she removes the barriers that defined the spirituality of men and women in different terms. The importance of this is that Julian did not await an eternal transition to establish equality between men and women, but illustrated that in the Christ-life here and now there need be "neither male nor female". All, as she says, are "partners with God". At least some of her contemporaries found no obstacle in accepting her as representing male and female alike, though it is indeed highly probable that many others looked askance on such an unconventional claim. For our times Julian stands as a forerunner of the ideal that women, while revering relationships, find their identity in themselves, and not in dependence on another.

The Mother Wisdom image thus transcends gender stereotypes, without disregarding the reality of male and female. The image is not a form of androgyny but is of a unique order, suggesting the restoring of both men and women to full humanity. Mother Wisdom is a God in whom there is both male and female, as father and mother, and in whom at the same time there is neither male nor female. We are the image of that God. In this paradox the motherhood of God in Julian rests.[22]

## Endnotes

1. *Julian of Norwich, Revelations of Divine Love,* trans. Clifton Wolters (Baltimore, Md., Penguin Books, 1973) 169.
2. Elizabeth Schuller, "Wisdom Mythology and the Christological Hymns of the New Testament", in Robert L. Wilken, ed. *Aspects of Wisdom of Judaism and Early Christianity* (Notre Dame, Ind., University of Notre Dame, 1975) 17 (Cited in Ritamary Bradley, "Patristic Backgrounds of the Motherhood Similitude in Julian of Norwich", *Christian Scholar's Review* 8:104).
3. *In Memory of Her A Feminist Theological Reconstruction of Christian Origins* (New York, Crossroad, 1983) 134.
4. *ST* I.I.ques. 45, art. 6, ad. 2. In the *Catena Aurea* Aquinas transmits traditional uses of the motherhood analogy by citing texts from Augustine and John Chrysostom. They say that the wisdom of God is our mother. *In Matthei Evangelium,* 23, *Quatuor Evangelia, Catena Aurea* (Marietti, 1938) 372.
5. For other texts see Ritamary Bradley, "Patristic Background of the Motherhood Similitude in Julian of Norwich", *Christian Scholar's Review* 8 (1978): 101–13; and especially Caroline Bynum, *Jesus as Mother: Studies in the Spirituality of the High Middle Ages* (Berkeley and Los Angeles, University of California Press, 1982) 125–129.
6. Caroline Bynum in *Jesus as Mother* believes that Julian adheres to these stereotypes, which she summarizes as follows: "The female is generative (the foetus is made of her very matter) and sacrificial in her generation (birth pangs)...; the female is loving and tender (the mother cannot help loving her own child); the female is nurturing (she feeds the child with her own bodily fluid)." 131.

7. Jeffrey Hamburger, "The Cor Ihesu as the Fons Sapientiae", in *The Rothschild Canticles: Art and Mysticism in Flanders and the Rhineland circa 1300* (New Haven and London, Yale University Press, 1990), especially p. 78.
8. Hamburger 78. He cites the *Speculum Virginum*, the visions of Elizabeth of Schonau and of Mechthild of Magdeburg, as well as *The Rothschild Canticles*.
9. Hamburger 78.
10. *Scale of Perfection*, Bk Two, chapter 39, 277–78. Note 293 by the editors (Clark and Dorward) says: "This section goes beyond the careful teaching of St. Thomas, ST 2-2, q. 26, aa. 7-8 with its respect for natural ties. But it does accord with the words of St. Bernard, *In Cant.* 50, 2.8."
11. *Ancrene Riwle* 162.
12. Grace M. Jantzen, *Julian of Norwich Mystic and Theologian* (New York, Paulist Press, 1988) 114.
13. Jantzen 118.
14. Jantzen 118.
15. Schüssler Fiorenza 135.
16. Schüssler Fiorenza135.
17. "The Spirit as God's Femininity", *Theology Digest* 30 (Summer, 1982): 130. From "Sur la maternité en Dieu et la fémininité du Saint-Esprit", *Escritos del Vedat* 11 (1981): 115–24.
18. Jurgen Moltmann, "The Motherly Father. Is Trinitarian Patripassionism Replacing Theological Patriarchalism?" in *God as Mother*, ed. Johannes-Baptist Metz and Edward Schillebeeckx Consilium Series (New York, Seabury Press, 1981) 53.
19. Moltmann 53.
20. *Selected Poetry of Jessica Powers*, ed. Regina Siegfried and Robert Morneau (Kansas City, Sheed and Ward, 1989) 138.
21. Rosemary Radford Ruether, *To Change the World: Christology and Cultural Criticism* (New York, Crossroad, 1990) 50.
22. "God(ess) restores both men and women to full humanity. The God(ess) who is both male and female, and neither male nor female, points us to an unrealized new humanity. In this

expanding image of God(ess) we glimpse our own expanding human potential, as selves and as social beings, that have remained truncated and confined in patriarchal, hierarchical relationships." Rosemary Radford Ruether, "The Female Nature of God: A Problem in Contemporary Religious Life", *God as Father*. Consilium, ed. Johannes-Baptist Metz and Edward Schillebeeckx (New York: The Seabury Press, 1981), 66.

## GOD IS IN ALL

Most of all, Julian finds God in the experiences which make up everyday life and relationships, and sees also that the one she loves transcends all boundaries. In her is verified what Bede Griffiths says of those who follow beyond knowledge (without abandoning reason) to the way of love: "... as one grows in knowledge of the God within, one becomes increasingly aware of the God beyond".[1]

In the twelfth showing, Julian cannot contain her joy over God's pervasive presence in all rightful human depth experiences. God is joy, in familiar forms and in awesome ones, in life itself, in all that we truly desire. Or, in an echo of the revelation to Moses, God says, "I am the one who is":

> ... I was taught that our soul will never be at rest until
> we come to him knowing that he is the fullness of joy,
> familiarly and courteously so, and our true life. Our
> Lord Jesus often said: "I am ... I am ... I am what
> is highest; I am what you love; I am what you take
> delight in; I am the one you serve; I am the one for
> whom you long ... the one you desire, the one you
> keep in mind. I am all that is. I am what holy church

preaches and teaches; and I am the one who has shown myself to you (LT 26).

There is more, she says, for in this message is included—and then she breaks off hindered by the weakness of language, overwhelmed by the memory of what she has realized. But she expects each of us to hear a similar message in our own way. When the heart is really at peace and at rest or touched by joy, there is God.

These are experiences of God in creation and in the deepest point of the self. On this foundation Julian shows us the way to God.

## Endnotes

1. Bede Griffiths, *A New Vision of Reality, Western Science, Eastern Mysticism and Christian Faith* (London, HarperCollins, 1989) 242.

# IV

# WHAT IS JULIAN'S WAY TO GOD?

## CONTRITION: SIN AND EVIL

Contrition—effective sorrow for our sin leading us to repentance—is one of the foundations of Julian's way. We are called to contrition, but not to shame, distress, and despair.

Julian understands how difficult it is to believe that God works by mercy and grace, without wrath. Often we insist on clinging to a punishing image of God: as if all sorrow that enters our life is God's chastising hand. Rather than admit that we often stumble into sin stupidly and blindly, we take comfort in an image of ourselves as always acting deliberately and with full awareness—and therefore when pain befalls us, we believe that we deserve to be severely punished. But while we are mistakenly thinking that God is angry, the Holy Ghost stirs us to contrition and with a desire to amend our lives (LT 40). Our shame shifts to what we have done to the image of God which we are—the image of power, wisdom, and love which we have gone contrary to and dimmed. We also want to blame our neighbours for their sins, instead of sharing contrition with them and grieving for their pain (LT 40).

God deals with us as if we had been in prison. On our release God speaks to us with affectionate words: "My darling, I was with you throughout that ordeal, and now we are one in bliss" (LT 40). Even today prison connotes human degradation, withdrawal of basic freedoms, miserable conditions, isolation, the company of others condemned by society and sometimes by their own conscience, and despair. What a picture Julian must have had of prison life. Even today the sanitized, museum-like dungeon of the old castle in Norwich is chilling and frightening. How it must have reeked of filth, outcries, and misery in Julian's time. Such is her image of sin and its effects.

Since God's love for us is never broken, our love for ourselves and for one another should never break down either (LT 40). Julian's message is one of pure love: we are to hate sin and to love others with a God-like love. Thus is the image of God in us restored.

## Lessons on Sin

Assuming this understanding of contrition, Julian deals (1) with sin and its kinds; (2) with sin as "naught"; and (3) with evil and the demonic.

*What is Sin?* Though Julian always extends comfort, she has anything but a soft teaching on sin. She says firmly: "... we are sinners, and do much evil that we ought not to do, and leave much undone that we ought to do" (LT 46). Sin is "a falling into ourselves" away from the sight of God. There we find no sense of being right, but only perversity. This condition springs from the "old root" of our oneness with the whole race, which fell in the beginning, and from the consent and nurturing we give this condition of our own will (LT 47). We add compost to the wild and infertile shoots of our nature.

In questioning how all shall be well, given such circumstances, Julian is taught to see sin—not as a list of transgressions—but as a fall, occasioned by human blindness. Sin is always considered in the context of the redeeming passion of Christ, and of our pain, and its restorative effects:

> In this naked word "sin" our Lord brought to my mind
> generally all that is not good, and the shameful
> contempt and utter noughting that he bore for us in
> this life; and his dying, and all the pains and sufferings,
> in body and spirit, of all his creatures. For we are all
> in part noughted, and we shall be until we are fully
> purged—that is, till we be fully noughted of our mortal
> flesh, and of our inward affections that are not very
> good (LT 27).

She takes care to exclude from the category of sin those instabilities which come from our physical nature. For an example she admits her sense of regret that she had asked to be close to the crucified Christ, now that she knows what suffering it entails. But this was not sin:

> ... now I could recognize it for what it was: the natural
> demurring and reaction of the body. My soul was not
> protesting, nor was God blaming me. I was experiencing
> both regret and deliberate choice at one and the same
> time. And this was due to the two sides of our nature,
> outward and inward. The outward side is our mortal,
> physical nature, which will continue to suffer and grieve
> all the time it lives—as I knew only too well! It was
> this part of me that regretted it all. The inward side
> is exalted and joyful and vital, all peaceful and loving.
> And deep down I was experiencing this. It was this part
> of me that so strongly, sensibly and deliberately chose
> Jesus for my heaven (LT 19).[1]

155

It should not be thought that Julian is here slipping back into a dualistic view of human nature as divided between a mortal body and an immortal soul. Rather, she is thinking of that part of us that is affected by the body. She refers here to a common experience—where one is at peace with a difficult choice, while still feeling the painful consequences of that choice. It is analogous to suffering the loss of a loved one without in any way rebelling against God's ways that have allowed the loved one to be separated from us, or even to die. She distinguishes between the "darkness of sin" and the "weight" of our body—both hindrances in different ways (LT 72).

God reveals our sin so that we see it "to our profit but without despair":

> Our Lord in his mercy shows us our sin and our
> weakness by the sweet, gracious light of himself; for
> our sin is so vile and so horrible that he of his courtesy
> will not show it to us but by the *light* of his grace and
> mercy (LT 78).

Sin is known by the pain (LT 27). But not all pain points to a corresponding transgression, no more than every movement of joy denotes an action that merits reward. Sometimes God allows personal limitations which bring down on us contempt, ridicule, and scorn—even exile. From her own experience Julian cites an instance in which she suffers interior pain without fault:

> For the profit of his soul, a man is sometimes left to
> himself, although sin is not always the cause. For at
> this time, the seventh showing, I sinned not, whereby
> I should be left to myself—for it came on me so
> suddenly. Neither did I deserve the blissful feeling. For

156

freely our Lord gives when he wills, and allows us at
times to be in woe (LT 15).

*Kinds of Sins:* Most treatises of Julian's time present lists of
sins, abstractly and systematically. We see this practice in
Chaucer's Parson's Tale, and in the *Myrour of Recluses*, and
to a certain degree in the *Ancrene Riwle*. Such treatises gave
attention especially to sins of the flesh about which Julian
says next to nothing, only that: "the desire of the flesh without consent is no sin" (LT 19). Even here, she is speaking
inclusively about any desire which does not look towards
God, not alone about lust.

In the course of the treatise Julian names the sins that relate
to her own experience and to the way of life she recommends.
Again, unlike many of her contemporaries, Julian does not
gather sins under the heading of disobedience; nor does she
link the types of sins to the misuse of the five senses.[2] Neither
does she follow the traditional listing of the seven (or eight)
capital sins. For herself and for those with whom she identifies
when she speaks of her even-Christians, the most dangerous
ways to sin are by sloth (*accidie*, sometimes related to
impatience), and despair.[3]

*Pride, Presumption, and Vainglory:* But before she elaborates
on these sins which threaten the lives of those intently seeking
God, she has something to say about pride, which is a peril
for all. By pride the creature would exalt himself above human
limitations. In the short text she accuses herself of pride for
her questioning of why sin was allowed. Why did not God
in his wisdom disallow sin and consequently prevent all the
pain which followed? (ST 13). She desperately wants all things
to be well. But in the long text she does not reproach herself
for her desire to understand how this can be, but continues
to converse with God about the gnawing difficulty. In fact,

insecurity about God's wisdom is precipitated almost in spite of ourselves by the spectacle of horrible and incomprehensible evil:

> ... [There are] evil deeds done in our sight which cause such great harm that it seems to us that it is impossible that they could ever come to a good end. We look on this, sorrowing and mourning for such things, so much so that we cannot be at rest in beholding God as we should do. But the cause is this: that the use of our reason is now so blinded, so low, and so undeveloped that we cannot know the high, marvellous wisdom and the power and the goodness of the blessed Trinity (LT 32).

She reserves the word "pride" for the sin of Satan and his followers. If we choose to join the devil's company, we share in the hatred and envy which leave him forever frustrated. But pride is also an underlying disposition to which humans are susceptible. Through the pain that follows on sin Christ works to eradicate such pride by leading us to relinquish respect for the "pomp and vainglory of this wretched life" (LT 28). As in the gospel where he likens himself to a mother hen in his longing to gather under his wings the citizens of Jerusalem who murder the prophets, Christ says:

> I will break you altogether from your vain affections and your vicious pride; and after that I shall gather you together and make you mild and meek, clean and holy, by making you one with me (LT 28).

Our sinful stances rooted in pride and presumption, its expression (LT 78), signify that we ignore our need for God. It is only by confronting us gently with our sins, making us feel ashamed, that God removes pride from our life. We come to know that without God we are only sin and wretchedness. By such painful but merciful enlightenment, "we shall be broken down as regards our pride and presumption" (LT 78).

Yet faithfully Julian recites and does not question what she has been taught by the medieval church, believing that it is based on God's word: the angels fell through pride and became fiends. They and some men on earth are damned:

> One point of our faith is that many creatures shall be damned, such as the angels that fell from heaven for pride, which are now devils; and men on earth who die outside the faith of holy church—that is, the heathen, and those who have received Christendom and yet live an unchristian life and die without charity, as holy church teaches me to believe (LT 32).

The church in her time would have ruled it an act of pride to take any exception to the range of such teaching, even that "the heathen" are destined for hell. But though Julian accepts the teaching, she admits she finds the scope of this doctrine hard to reconcile with the promise of her showings that "all shall be well". She did not foresee that the church to which she adhered would, six centuries later, repudiate all forms of discrimination against peoples because of their religion.[4] This would imply withholding judgment on their standing before God. Such opening to others may be one step towards making all things well, in fact. But even at that, some great deed needs to be done to enable us to see how sin was necessary and fitting.

*Sloth and Despair*: Despite these passing comments on pride, and on its accompanying expressions of vainglory and presumption, Julian notes that she saw sin only in general—except for sloth or impatience, and despair. She speaks of both of these as forms of sickness (LT 73). By despair, one could fall so low as to lose all sight of God's love. By sloth, or recklessness, one could risk a fall, by acting as if nothing matters, forgetting that "we may not stand for the twinkling of an eye unless we be upheld by grace" (LT 52).

These categories resemble in striking ways the analysis of sin arrived at by Søren Kierkegaard.[5] Hence, exploring his analysis of sin leads us more deeply into Julian's meaning.

Kierkegaard sums up all sin as despair. But he breaks despair into two parts, the first of which is only improperly called despair.[6] It is like the medieval concept of sloth or spiritual torpor, to which Julian refers. The second resembles Julian's concept of doubting dread.[7] In its most malevolent form, it is a denial of and a revolt against the goodness of existence.[8] Kierkegaard, too, discerns both these sins to be a sickness which requires healing by the divine physician.

*Sloth or Impatience—A Form of Despair*: Sloth is essentially an indifference to the call to live one's faith radically. The first sign of sloth is rejection of the way of suffering: bearing travail and pain with resentment. Sloth is a failure to incorporate the patience of Christ on the cross into a life which necessarily includes some sorrow and pain. The seeming absence of God requires patience, as does also the uncertainty about when life will end. But the slothful one lives in the categories of agreeable/disagreeable, having bid goodbye to truth, which is the index of spirit.[9] When seeking God becomes troublesome, less pleasant, we fall away from wilfully and busily seeking (LT 10).

Sloth dims the divine perspective in life and blinds a person not only to God but to the self in which God lives.

Kierkegaard calls this state of soul narrowness. Instead of

measuring life by divine norms, the narrow, or shallow, person takes something indifferent in value as an idol, and loses connectedness with all humanity: "... by becoming wise about how things go in this world, such a man forgets himself, forgets what his name is (in the divine understanding of it), does not dare to believe in himself, finds it too venturesome a thing to be himself, far easier and safer to be like the others, to become an imitation, a number, a cipher in the crowd."[10] The slothful person lives in the parrot-wisdom of trivial experience. Deceived by the joys of life or by its sorrows, such a one "may never become eternally and decisively conscious of himself as spirit".[11] Such lack of action is, unfortunately, not always recognized as sin:

> To be in the strictest sense a sinner is ... very far from
> being meritorious. But then on the other hand how on
> earth can one expect to find an essential consciousness
> of sin (and after all, that is what Christianity wants)
> in a life which is so retarded by triviality, by a
> chattering imitation of "the others", that one hardly
> can call it sin, that it is too spiritless to be so called,
> and fit only, as the Scripture says, to be "spewed out"?[12]

Sloth also carries the common meaning of a failure in alacrity in doing good. Kierkegaard says this is what makes sloth a sin: because the good must be done at once, as soon as it is known; or the intelligence will become obscured.[13] When one dallies over following the enlightenment in the intellect until the moment of grace passes, the will becomes corrupted. A state of torpor follows.

In terms of modern culture, as Kierkegaard presents it, to be spiritually apathetic sometimes involves being secure in legal righteousness. Or it may take the form of satisfaction with this world's view of success, and not even be thought of as "loss of self":

> This form of despair is hardly ever noticed in the world. Such a man, precisely by losing his self in this way, has gained perfectibility in adjusting himself to business, yea, in making a success in the world ... he is ground smooth as a pebble, courant as a well-used coin. So far from being considered in despair, he is just what a man ought to be. In general the world has, of course, no understanding of what is truly dreadful. The despair which not only occasions no embarrassment but makes one's life easy and comfortable is naturally not regarded as despair.[14]

Apathy in the medieval sense is also close to what Karl Rahner calls concupiscence. It is "the tendency of the dallying spirit to postpone its own recovery, to delay its return ..." It is a state "in which the higher powers go limp and surrender to the desires seated in the lower powers".[15] Julian is on the edge of such apathy when "because of a little pain" she temporarily denies the reality of her revelations. She attributes to sloth her impatience with life: distressed with her wretchedness and weakness, she says: "I did not want to live and toil as it falls to us to do" (LT 64).

Sloth is resistance to growth, the failure to do what we are capable of doing. The only way to be free of sloth—of this form of despair—is to be transparently grounded in the Power which has made us, preserves us, and loves us.

*Despair or Doubting Dread*: Sloth is linked to the despair that is doubting dread by the action of the fiend. In Julian's case he seems to have berated her with her past failings, accusing her of losing time and of making promises which she did not keep (LT 76). He tries to overwhelm her with the sight of real and imagined weaknesses.

Despair would lead us to deny that life has an ultimate meaning, that it possesses an essential goodness and purpose. Despair is unbelief in the impossible that only God can do. Despair denies that God does, in fact, act beyond our power to act.

Here, too, Kierkegaard is remarkably helpful in elucidating what is implied by despair as Julian sees it. The slothful person does not realize that he is in despair over the eternal, as he pursues other goals, only half-heartedly regarding God. But in doubting dread a person is disheartened specifically over her weakness and seeming inability to reach God. She believes that she has irretrievably lost the eternal and lost herself:

> The despairer understands that it is weakness to take
> the earthly so much to heart, that it is weakness to
> despair. But then, instead of veering sharply away from
> despair to faith, humbling himself before God for his
> weakness, he is more deeply absorbed in despair, and
> despairs over his weakness.[16]

Pain also can bring us to the verge of "moaning and despair". But to avert this:

> He [Christ] wants us to know that we do not suffer
> alone but with him; that he is our ground; and that
> his pains and his self-emptying so far surpass anything
> we could suffer that we can never comprehend it (LT 28).

Julian's medicine for this state of despair is to know that the voice of God says always: "I keep you securely" (LT 40). This is true even in the midst of other sin.

# Julian's Way

## Sin is Naught

Finally, then, what is sin? Sin, Julian emphasizes, is all that is not good (LT 27). On the way to God, sin is a fall, as she shows in relation to the parable of the Lord and the Servant. But its causes, described in images, are blindness, darkness, contrariness, frailty, sickness, paralysis, a coma, all of which can precipitate a literal fall.

Sin has no reality, no goal. It is like speech that has no meaning; like a story "told by an idiot", it brings no bliss. In its vacuity it promises by appearances, and disappoints by its residue of pain. It is the most shameful scourge we can be smitten with (LT 39). Just as the lie has no truth, deceit partakes of no friendship, so sin is not founded in being. Because it is not grounded in being, it is nothing: it is like a screw driven into bog, or into moldy earth, which cannot hold.[17] Or it is like temporary interference on a television screen, which vanishes when order is restored. "I saw not sin for I believe it has no substance, no part of being; and it would not be known if it were not for the pain it causes" (LT 27).

For today's reader, not immersed in the philosophical refinements of the Middle Ages, the notion that sin is nothing is hard to comprehend. But Julian is working from experience, and understands her showings in terms of experience, helped by reason, and safeguarded by faith.

Furthermore, we must always remember that Julian sees from the double perspective of time and eternity—not separate but interwoven, like the music on the page and the living music being achieved. When she says sin is naught, she means, in part, that it will come to nothing. When a person deliberately chooses sin, *in the end* he has nothing (ST 18). Sin has been annihilated by God's suffering. The passion has made it to be nothing. Like the way of the wicked, it vanishes. In this light, we find it easier to understand, without undue recourse to paradox, that sin indeed is nothing.

How is evil to be opposed? Christ has taught us to do good against evil (ST 18). But evil ought not to be projected outward, for it is within ourselves, when we add to its force by cooperating.

Julian does not set out to fight evil—as if she is good and the fiends are evil—but has recourse to the passion, which has overcome evil. Evil is not like two hands that are beating against each other, one evil and the other good; but rather like cold or pain inseparable from both hands, crippling and weakening the hands. It can only be eased by a joining of the two hands, gently flexing and warming each other until the pain eases, and the cause of the pain ceases.

Nor is sin and evil in the neighbour a reason for refusing to love our even-Christians. Julian counsels hatred of sin both in ourselves and in others, without allowing such hatred to flow over onto the person who sins.

Julian's treatise is mostly about goodness and very little about evil (LT 33). Nonetheless, she was not drawn to deny the doctrines she had been taught about hell and purgatory. Yet when she desires to see these, her request, we will recall, is not fulfilled. The divine teacher wanted her to base her motivations on love, rather than on fear of punishment.

She comes close to knowing about hell, however, in the two demonic temptations. The assaults take place in a dream, but the aftermath of that dream is a temptation to sloth and despair.

## Evil and the Demonic

The demonic assaults are in two parts. In the first the demon seems about to strangle her, which signifies that he will try to block her from speaking of her visions.

The attack is like a rape. She feels overpowered. She resists with all her might, yet knows she cannot be safe without the help of others. Her experience epitomizes all the violence attempted on women in particular, whether on their body or spirit, or by their being reduced to powerlessness in the ecclesiastical and social order. The attacker is not a man but ugly, disembodied power, just as patriarchy is. It arouses feelings of revulsion.

The attack contrasts sharply with the demonic seductions reported by desert fathers. For them the seducer is usually an apparition of a beautiful woman, or an abstraction of femininity, enticing the hermit to sexual excess—perhaps to overpowering another. Julian's attacker is deformed and less than human. There is nothing attractive in it, and she is moved only to resistance.

After this first assault, Julian converses briefly with those around her, recognizes the fiend as an emissary of evil, and fixes her heart intently on the memory of her showings. Uppermost, perhaps, might have been the sixth showing (LT 14), which had also come to her mind in connection with the parable of the lord and the servant. There, after Christ had assured her that he scorned the fiend, she had seen a peaceful vision rich in sensory detail. The lord was seated as a host in his own house. He was surrounded by friends whose service he wished to acclaim, and his love was like a "marvellous, never-ending melody". The divine host is now a king, who has made in her heart "his home where he is most at home, and his dwelling from which he will never depart" (LT 67). Again, the divine king is not battling with Satan, but peacefully ruling and guiding heaven and earth and all that exists. Comforted, Julian returns to her true calling: to behold the goodness of God.

But after the second phase of the assault, she almost succumbs to both sloth and despair. It is not that she does not resist this temptation, too, for she clings to her trust in God and comforts herself with prayers. But the struggle is more intense. The prayers being recited lovingly at her side are so distorted in her dream that they seem to have no meaning. She counters the fiend with her whole being, fixating her physical eye on the cross, repeating to herself the story of the passion and the truths of faith, and setting the eye of her heart on God in trust. But the thought comes to her that she is presumptuous to focus on God's goodness as she has just been taught. She wonders if she should not make the avoidance of sin her main business—taking it not only as a good occupation but as a "sovereign", all-encompassing one. Her attention has shifted away for the moment from the fact that she could not keep herself from sin simply by willing to do so, nor by her own power. The fiend penetrates into her consciousness at this point, taking advantage of her by confusion. He has made her forget the lesson of the first showing: "He wills that we be occupied in knowing and loving till that time when we will be fulfilled in heaven" (LT 6).

Then she is drawn to the brink of despair when, we may suppose, the fiend taunts her with her weakness. Has she not often broken her promises to God in the past, and has she forgotten her daily sins? (LT 73). Thus, like a rapist he seems to suggest to her that she has brought the assault on herself, has implicitly invited him to take possession of her.

In some ways he does take possession of her bodily powers. The stench "keeps her very busy", probably because it induces nausea. The "bodily heat" keeps her occupied, fighting off the effects of fever. The chattering "business" of the two bodies diffuses her consciousness and annoys her. She

167

counters cleverly with some "bodily" business of her own. She addresses herself, in audible speech, with the words of comfort she would have spoken to help another in similar circumstances. This "bodily business", which is ensouled by grace, and lets her think of others, puts all the other activity in its place. By this creative strategy she circumvents the trap by which the fiend would imprison her in her own misery. She regains a presence of mind, and escapes from being totally absorbed in bodily functions.

Thus she makes a transition. Though she will still try to avoid sin, her life is to be primarily focused on beholding the goodness of God. Pursuing that "business", she will not see her weakness in a discouraging light.

*A Word in Her Memory*: But though the stink of the fiend lingers on, as a token of the demonic presence, there is no sign nor token left of the blissful showings. All that is left is a word in her understanding. In her memory there lingers the merry, sweet face of God, fully human.

> All this sorrow that he causes us to have, it shall be turned back on him. It was for this that our Lord scorned him; and this made me mightily to laugh (LT 77).

She can return to the fifth showing and to that prayer "in the simplicity of her heart", wherein she savoured the truth that the fiend is overcome by the power of the passion. Likewise, she can take comfort again in the eighth showing, where she keeps her gaze on Christ, because without the cross there is no protection against the horror of the fiends.

## *"May Your Hearts be Ever Merry!"*

Up to this time Julian had spoken of two kinds of knowing necessary to us: first, that we know our Lord God; and second, that we know our self, which entails understanding what we are by nature and grace. After the temptations she realistically adds a third: that we meekly know ourselves with regard to our sin and weakness (LT 72). The wound that she had asked for first is given to her in its fullness last.

Thus, contrition removes sin, and trust fends off evil and the demonic. She has retraced the psalmist's prayer. (Psalm 22). It, too, begins with a cry of abandonment ("My God, my God, why have you forsaken me?"); it moves on to a prayer for protection ("Save me from the lion's mouth ... my wretched life"); and ends in re-dedication to the goodness of God, to an awareness of others, and to the experience of joy:

> "They who seek the LORD shall praise him;
> 'May your hearts be ever merry!'" (Psalm 22:27).

## Endnotes

1. *Julian of Norwich: Revelations of Divine Love*, trans. Clifton Wolters (Baltimore, Md., Penguin Books, 1973), 93.
2. A typical example appears in *The Myrour of Recluses*, a Middle English translation of the *Speculum Inclusorum*, ed. Marta Powell Harley. Typescript. Part I, chapter 3.
3. Hilton follows this traditional listing: pride, envy, wrath, *accidie*, covetousness, gluttony and lechery (Bk. I, chapt. 55). In a note to this passage (p. 176, note 230), Clark and Dorward trace this listing to Peter Lombard, *Sentences*, Book 2, distinction 42, c. 6, "on the basis of Gregory, *Moralia* 31–45.87". They note early occurrences of a listing of seven (or eight) capital sins in Evagrius Ponticus, *Prakitos*; and Cassian, *Collationes*, Book 5. Regarding sloth, they write: "*Accidie* derives from the Greek ... and is a technical term referring to disinclination

to any spiritual activity.... In English it is sometimes represented by 'sloth'."

4. "Declaration on the Relationship of the Church to Non-Christian Religions", in *The Documents of Vatican Council II* (New York, Guild Press, 1966) 660–668.
5. Søren Kierkegaard, *Fear and Trembling and the Sickness Unto Death*, trans. Walter Lowrie (Garden City, N.Y., Doubleday and Co., 1954). Søren Kierkegaard, born in Copenhagen in 1813, died there in 1855. He is considered the father of contemporary philosophy.
6. Kierkegaard 6.
7. Kierkegaard 175–207.
8. Kierkegaard 207.
9. Kierkegaard 176.
10. Kierkegaard 166.
11. Kierkegaard 159–60.
12. Kierkegaard 232.
13. Kierkegaard 225.
14. Kierkegaard 167.
15. Robert E. Doud, "Placing Rahner, Interpreting Roethke", *Religion and Literature* 16 (Autumn, 1984), 52.
16. Kierkegaard 195.
17. Kierkegaard 232.

# COMPASSION

Julian's concept and experience of compassion deepens and expands in a remarkable progression. Initially it is narrow and devotional, concerned with her personal feeling as a co-sufferer with Christ crucified. The icon of this desire was the gathering of the devout women at the foot of the cross, weeping for the bloodshed and pain they beheld in the sinless one whom they loved. Her associates in her contemplation were to be limited to these friends of Jesus in his lifetime.

As her perspective on compassion changes, it is transformed. She comes to contemplate the compassion of Christ, with less attention to her own exercise of compassion. And her own compassion broadens to include Christ and his people, as one body with him. In the process of growth she comes to see the connection between compassion and self-emptying or noughting, with Christ as her model.

*Her Bodily Feeling of Christ's Pain*: By her preliminary prayer for the wound of natural compassion Julian meant that she desired a bodily feeling of sharing in Christ's pains (LT 2). With the first showing she focuses on the suffering caused by the garland of thorns, and she does indeed feel compassion for the suffering Christ, as she recognizes him as the one who suffered most for her. Yet this compassion—this suffering with Christ—is accompanied by unspeakable joy, which indeed overflows into love for her even-Christians. However, the love is not yet specified as compassion for those others (LT 6). And though she sees Mary, she does not at this point see her overwhelmed with grief. Rather, she sees "our blessed lady" at the time of Christ's conception, and she looks on her wrapped in wonder at the condescension of God in coming to a lowly creature.

With the eighth showing her sharing in Christ's bodily pain is so intense, so all-absorbing, that it displaces all other pain. She admits that she regrets, at the level of feeling, that she ever asked for such an experience. It is at this point that she has a vision of Mary at the foot of the cross and sees a part of her compassion (LT 18). But mysteriously Mary is understood, not simply as a mother in grief, but as the epitome and summation of a natural compassion (supremely augmented by grace), which all those called to salvation have.

171

In fact, the whole visible universe of creatures shares in its own way in this natural compassion. In a special degree, those people who knew not Christ were in sorrow for him, too. No longer is Julian's compassion what she had dreamed of—a special experience limited to those devout women present at the crucifixion and to those who might ask to share in it. Because of her connectedness with all other bodily creatures, she realizes that they, too, have a share in the very sufferings of Christ. She is part of the earth's body. And as part of the body of sinful creatures, she is taught to behold the pains of Christ "with contrition and compassion" (LT 21).

## The Compassion of Christ

(a) *Because of Sin*: In the thirteenth showing to the end, there is an about face in what Julian means by compassion. She comes to understand "Christ" differently—as to who he is, how he suffers, and from whence compassion springs.

Her attention is directed away from the compassion of creatures, to the compassion of Christ himself: the very meaning of the compassion of Christ also undergoes a change, as she tells us. For in the teaching she had had before the showings, she had understood that divine mercy consisted in God's turning away from the wrath that he had for us because of our sin (LT 47). But in the course of the showings she learns how it is that Christ exercises compassion for the sinner (LT 28). As the mother gives all for the child, so the suffering Jesus excuses us and "regards us with compassion and pity, like children, innocent and loved" (LT 28). In this co-mingling of compassion and pity, he lays on all who are "the children of salvation" some pain that is not sinful. This is done so

172

that when others despise them, they will not be drawn to the pomp and vain acclaim of this wretched world. We are further consoled by knowing that we do not suffer alone, but with Christ.

Julian, too, is then moved from an attitude of simple love to compassion. She is "fulfilled in part with compassion for all her even-Christians" (LT 28). This compassion extends not only to individuals but includes what happens to the corporate body of God's well-beloved people, his servants, the church: "[It] shall be shaken by sorrows and anguish and tribulation in this world as men shake a cloth in the wind" (LT 28).

Christ's compassion extends to our vain efforts to know the counsel hidden in divine providence (LT 30), helping us to realize, instead, that his wisdom and love will not let the end come until the best time (LT 31). His compassion will endure until the day of judgement, when it will cease, for then his thirst for us will have been fulfilled (LT 31). Until that time he also exercises his compassion, not only towards us, but through us:

> And then I saw that every act of natural compassion
> that a man has for his even-Christians, it is Christ in
> him (LT 28).

This Christ-life is exercised in particular when the Christian is confronted with the sins of others. Julian directs us, not to condemn, but to share compassion with the other, cognizant of our own weakness:

> If a soul will be at rest, when other men's sins come
> into his mind, he shall flee from the sight as from the
> pain of hell, seeking in God remedy and help. For
> beholding of another man's sin, creates, as it were, a

173

thick mist before the eye of the soul; and we may not
for the time see the fairness of God—unless we may
behold that other with contrition along with him, with
*compassion on him*, and with a holy desire unto God
for him (LT 76).

(b) *Christ's Compassion for Our Pain*: Christ's compassion
is not just for our sin and our folly, but extends also to our
pain. This pain may spring from the sharpened sense of our
own limitations, which make us liable to sin. Christ permits
this pain, for suffering has a role in fostering compassion
and in preparing us for God's new gifts (LT 39).

But what of the pain that comes to us without any blame,
simply from the human condition? In the fifteenth showing,
in the vision of the innocent child transformed from wretchedness to glory, Julian sees the compassion Christ has for
all our pain:

It is a supreme comfort and a blissful sight for a loving
soul to know that we shall be taken from pain. For
in this promise I saw the marvellous compassion that
our Lord has for us in our woe; and I received a
courteous assurance of total deliverance. For he wills
that we be comforted to the uttermost (LT 64).

This compassion takes shape as comfort, fostered with
Christ's words:

And you will come up above; and you will have me
for your reward; and you will be fulfilled in joy and
bliss (LT 64).

## Compassion and Self-Emptying

Compassion is the correlative, the other side, of "noughting", or self-emptying. Christ himself exemplifies this connection: "The same *noughting* that was shown in his passion, it was shown here again (in the 13th showing) *in this compassion* ..." [LT 28]).

Scripture refers to Christ's "noughting" in terms of his emptying himself by taking the form of a servant (Phil. 2:7). Theologians have frequently seen this self-emptying as the willing renouncing of the glory of his divinity in the taking on of the humiliation of the human condition.[1] But Julian seems to be describing the "noughting" as the pouring out of the lifestream of his blood, thus emphasizing his total self-giving in his humanity out of compassion.

After seeing the compassion of Christ, she comes to know her Self—the transcendent Self—which is achieved through "noughting". When the ego-self steps aside, the transcendent Self can take over consciousness, at least in part. Then we are united to all humanity as Christ was in the passion. As it is harder to know our Self than to know God, it is also harder to feel compassion for all others than for the innocent, sacrificing Christ.

In the matter of penance, as we have seen, Julian did not stress a penitential programme, but rather the acceptance of life as penance. Here, consistently, she does not offer an ascetical system for self-emptying. Rather, self-emptying follows on entering fully into life as it is. To love and accept this created world totally is to accept its suffering and to risk encounter with its evil.

Consistently, Julian sees noughting, or self-emptying, as the other side of compassion: self-emptying is achieved by the practice of compassion. Christ's individuality, too, gave

way in his Incarnation to an awareness that he was humanity
in its collective misery. And as death on the cross was indis-
tinguishable from Christ's rising into joy, so at the same
moment that self-emptying occurs in the individual, the
greater Self begins to be unveiled. This stepping aside of the
ego-self is therefore a stage of growth rather than of diminish-
ment. This is why Julian speaks of being "fulfilled" with
compassion, both for the pains of Christ crucified and for
her even-Christians.

Julian had been initiated into self-emptying in the hazelnut
vision (LT 5). There she had learned not to follow the ego-self
in clinging to creation but to look beyond appearances to
God who fills it and is our rest. But she later learns further
that compassion is the road to true union with God: "Each
act of natural compassion a man performs for his even-Christians in love is Christ in him." And in this compassion,
wherein the ego-self is transcended, it is also Christ continuing
his own "noughting" as experienced on the cross (LT 28).

Compassion reaches its fullness only when the ego-con-
sciousness has been transformed and made all one with humanity. This is expressed in a summary of the insights of Thomas
Merton, who found such profound wisdom in Julian. The
quest for God and the quest for the transcendent Self, while
not synonymous, are inseparable: "If I find Him [God] I
will find myself and if I find my true self I will find him":

> ... the discovery of the Transcendent Self has been
> termed the "transformation of consciousness." *The
> Transcendent Self can be described as "the No-one who has
> gone beyond the individual self by compassion and purity
> of love and humility, and who is, consequently, united
> with all."*[2]

Compassion is a commonly recognized component of mystical experience, in both Eastern and Western religious traditions. But it is held by some that the nature of that compassion is a key to distinguishing one tradition from another. Edward Schillebeeckx, for example, argues for that distinction:

> The religions of Eastern Asia are primarily religions of the inner life, even though they all have a very complex form of external ritual. There is no confrontation between man and the divine element, which is experienced as the ground of man's innermost self and at the same time the ground of the entire cosmos, in which plurality is experienced as unity. The divine is also regarded as impersonal or rather as suprapersonal, *as a mystery of compassion embracing everything.*[3]

Schillebeeckx sees the religions of Western Asia, including Christianity, as "sharply contrasted with those of the East" on the matter of humanity's sharing in responsibility for history out of compassion which thirsts for justice:

> Judaism, Christianity and Islam are all, I think, characterized by their emphasis on a personal God who speaks to man, questions him and challenges him. This confrontation that takes place between God and man in the West is done through prophets . . . . God makes man, who is created in his image, *responsible for history.* Man becomes himself in a historical confrontation with his God. He becomes an individual person who is free and who has the right to speak and even to speak with God. The classical example of this is, of course, the Old Testament figure of Job . . . . Jews, Christians and Muslims all have the task of establishing the kingdom of God as a kingdom of justice among men.[4]

Like Job before her, Julian confronts God with the problem of suffering, especially when it seems undeserved. Her love for her even-Christians, in their pain and illusions, is awakened in her first showing, and then matures into compassion. She perceives the role of all of us to be "partners with God" in the deed that will overcome the evil that has deformed the world.

Julian's treatise is thus not about a devout woman who mourns for the sorrows of the one she loves.

It is about the compassion of God.

Hence, as she nears a summing up of what she has learned in the showings, Julian says:

> When I say that he waits for us, sorrowing and
> mourning, it means:
>
>> —all the *contrition and compassion* that we have
>> within ourselves; and all sorrowing and mourning
>> that we are not yet one with our Lord.
>
> And all of this that is for our welfare; it is Christ
> in us.
>> And though some of us feel it only seldom,
>> it is always in Christ
>> until he has brought us out of all our woe.
> For unless there also be pity, there can never
> be love (LT 80).

## Endnotes

1. See footnote to Phil. 2:6 in *The Catholic Study Bible*, ed. Donald Senior, et al (New York and Oxford, Oxford University Press, 1990) 314: "Either a reference to Christ's preexistence and those aspects of divinity that he was willing to give up in order to

serve in human form, or to what the man Jesus refused to grasp at to attain divinity. Many see an allusion to the Genesis story: unlike Adam, Jesus, though ... in the form of God (Gen. 1:26–27), did not reach out for equality with God, in contrast with the first Adam in Gen. 3:5–6."

2. Virginia F. Randall, "The Mandala as Structure in Thomas Merton's *The Geography of Lograire*", *A Journal of Religion in Literature* 11 (Oct., 1978), 1–2.

3. Edward Schillebeeckx, *God is New Each Moment* (New York, The Seabury Press, 1983) 114.

4. Schillebeeckx 114. The question of likenesses and differences between Eastern and Western mystical traditions, of course, is a subject on which there is considerable difference of opinion among experts. But Schillebeeckx's remarks help to set Julian's position in relief. On this subject see also "Buddhist-Christian Dialogue: An Early Journey", *Bulletin 41*, North American Board for East–West Dialogue (May, 1991), 8–12.


# CLEAVING TO GOD

## *In Dread and Doubt, Fear, Love, and Trust*

A remarkable motif woven through the text and defining our way to God is the theme of *dread*.[1] How often, in those terrifying times of the fourteenth century, must not weary pilgrims and other heavy-hearted Christians found their way to Julian's cell for words of comfort and for guidance in discerning the movements of their hearts. Fear, which seems to threaten trust, to the contrary, in Julian's view, strengthens and solidifies it and becomes awe (LT 74).

She knew this, indeed, from experience. The prayer she offered in her youth included a petition for knowing all the fears and turmoil (*dredes* and tempests) that were associated with facing the fiends at the point of death (LT 2). Then in the final revelation after she had endured two assaults by the devils, she is able to call others and herself to self-forgiveness for fears that might seem to be blameworthy (LT 73). It is then that she composes a chapter explicitly on dread.

In that chapter (LT 74) Julian is most explicit when she speaks of feelings of dread experienced in the presence of God. Through the Scriptures she would have known that the women at the empty tomb were filled with this dread. Such dread is a gift of God. It is this fear, coupled with joy, that filled the hearts of the women who first met the risen Christ (Matt. 28). It means reverential fear or awe, analogous in some way to the awe inspired in us by sublime manifestations of nature, such as the mountains, the forests, and the sea. A similar feeling arises also in the presence of what seems to be holy—such as a place where we know heroic, loving, and prayer-centred lives have been lived, or a living person who embodies goodness and love. We are drawn to closeness, at the same time as we are deterred from violating or trying to possess that which inspires awe. When such dread is felt, it is a stance to be consciously and willfully cultivated and cherished. It brings with it peace and rest.

There are lesser forms of dread, which can be salutary, and counterfeit forms of dread, which can be destructive. The lesser forms are born of passion and imagination; the destructive forms can deceive us into believing they are feelings implanted in us by God. Synonyms for the other forms of fear range from uneasiness, through anxiety, doubt, fright, and even terror.

Though Julian gives us a chapter explicitly on the subject of *dread* in its several forms, her principal concern is with reverential fear. (1) This is presented throughout the text from her own experience and from her encounters with those who came to her for counselling. (2) She brings to a head in the chapter on dread how reverential fear differs from other forms. (3) Reverential fear is then further developed after that formal analysis.

## Julian's Experience of Reverential Fear

In the first showing (which, she reminds us, contains all the rest) reverential fear was a component of her beholding of God as the maker. Mingled with love, it brings about a salutary sense of the smallness of the creature (LT 5). The exemplar of reverential fear is Mary, who was fulfilled in awe as she waits in the presence of God (LT 7). From Mary she learns to know herself, while reverently fearing God (LT 25). And in that context she marvels that God who is so awe-inspiring is also so familiar and courteous (LT 7).

In this matter as elsewhere for Julian, experience is always complex. Though her contemporaries, especially in the drama, favoured isolating a single virtue, thinking of it abstractly, and even personifying it, she writes from a perspective of life as it is lived and felt. Hence, reverential fear is intertwined with other attitudes. Basically it is mingled with love. Again, though medieval Christian piety accepted quite universally that the presence of the Trinity is awe-inspiring, this attitude at times gave way to lesser feelings in the contemplation of the humanity of Christ. Not so for Julian. Fear is joined to sorrow in her sight of the lacerated flesh of Jesus, about to fall to the ground (LT 17). When mingled with such sorrow, fear may itself be painful—but then hope is the dominant component of the experience and restores comfort (LT 47). More explicitly, grace transforms our fearful feelings into endless solace (LT 48). In a summary observation, she notes that fear may be accompanied with four other work-ings: enjoying, sorrowing, desiring, and hoping (LT 47).

We can generalize from the explicit record of Julian's exper-iences about these workings of reverent fear. It is a component in the complex of responses she feels in the showings of the passion: perceiving that the flow of Christ's blood was as uncountable as drops of rain in a flash-flood, she thought the sight both "hideous and awe-inspiring" (LT 7). As she looks on the buffeted, bloodied face of Christ in his sufferings, her spirits are stirred with feelings of fear, along with sorrow and longing (LT 10). These, in turn, beget joy (LT 8). Some-times awe is muted and becomes a gentle, quiet fear, as when she beholds God in a point, seeing all the energies of the universe concentrated in the unextended convergence of inward power and outward manifestation (LT 11). This fear that God's presence begets is "sweet and delectable" (LT 65), creates a sense of security and can erase pain. It is accompanied at times with such comfort that even when pain persists, it is not disturbing. She tells us of such a time, when she herself felt so much comfort and rest that neither fear, nor sorrow, nor pain could disturb her (LT 15).

Reverent fear is a component of the forms of prayer Julian has taught us. In the prayer of thanking it manifests itself as inward knowing and takes the qualities of loving fear (LT 41). In the prayer of beholding, it interweaves with enjoying the self-disclosure of God (LT 43).

This feeling of awe, reverence, or fear is truly pervasive in Julian's relationship to God. A remarkable number of times she admits to this fear—always pointing in two directions: to her own weakness and to God's greatness. Often it simply means: "I was afraid..." She was afraid, for example, that the visions would cease before she was fully instructed, and that she would be left to herself (LT 47). Certainly it is her

182

personal experience that enables her to affirm: When the sight and feeling of God's presence leaves us, then we are filled with dread (LT 48).

It is deepest and most painful with regard to the effects of sin. Addressing God "with very great fear" she pleads to know: "How can all be well when such harm has come to creatures through sin?" (LT 29). When she realizes in God's presence that she and all others will sin, at least by weakness and mischief, she feels a "gentle fear"; but God reassures her with great love and tenderness (LT 37). With deeper feeling yet, she laments: "Our failing is *dreadful*; our falling is shameful; our dying is sorrowful" (LT 48). And in those unspeakably dark hours of sorrow, anguish, and tribulation that may be precursors of miracles, we again face our weakness and our mischief and are moved to fear (LT 36). But the sweet motherly eye of pity and mercy never ceases to regard us (LT 48). Indeed, such fear is salutary and makes us, by God's goodness, strenuously to seek forgiveness, laying our need before Mother Christ (LT 49, 63). Nor are spiritual enemies to be feared—only God—for all their might is locked in his hands (LT 65). After the nightmarish appearance of demons just before the end of the showings, even though they seemed to accuse her of sin and breaking of promises, she felt no fear in her conscience when she awakened (LT 66). Mother Jesus will not allow us to perish, though in the face of our wretchedness we are "sore adred" (LT 61).

But we also experience dread at the sight of God's mysterious workings—such as how harmoniously reason and faith are in accord (LT 83). And regarding what is to come, joy will permeate the awe that enlightens anyone who contemplates how, despite the ravages and horror of sin, God's goodness will unfold in the great deed by which all will be made well (LT 36).

## Other Kinds of Dread

Some kinds of dread arise apart from love and can take on the colour of holiness (LT 74). Yet even these can lead us to God as mother—by a magnetism, a guidance that is kind, gracious, good and true. Or if evil, such fears can be turned into good (LT 74).

1) One is fright, which comes on us suddenly because we are weak. It is the fear experienced in the presence of danger. This fear serves to purge us, just as does bodily sickness, or any other pain that is not the direct result of sin (LT 74). It is the fear that prompts a child to run to its mother (LT 63). In a more intense form, this was the fear witnessed at the crucifixion, when St. Denys, as Julian calls him, trembled before the sorrowful and fearful events then transpiring (LT 18). It is remarkable that Julian even conceives of Christ as suffering such fear: for "fright and dread" overtook the Servant in the face of his mission, prompting the Lord to ask: "Should I not reward my servant for such suffering?" (LT 51). And again, because he has taken on the garment of that flesh which has sinned, he fears to stand before the Lord. This fear fades, when he comes as transformed humanity, in the rich clothing—the wedding garment—of the new being (LT 51).

2) The next is the dread of pain, the fear of suffering to come. Such dread awakens us from the sleep of sin, which is like a coma, and makes it possible to overcome the fear of death and the power of demons. If we look back, we shall recall that it is this very pain which Julian prayed to pass through: to come to the point of death and to meet the demons that might threaten at that hour. She still believes that the fear of such pain is salutary—that it enables one to seek comfort and mercy from God, and to be open to

the grace of the Holy Ghost which leads to contrition.[2] Yet she had not been asleep in sin, given her desire to love God so intensely; still, she wished to overcome the fear of what might assault her at the hour of her dying. This fear never entirely left her, for she later admits that "sloth makes us fear to appear before God" (LT 76). When the fear of the consequences of sin was silent, another replaced it: a fear of what God would reveal to her. This, too, should be rejected. For she tells us—or perhaps herself—that we should not fear to know what God wills to disclose to us (LT 36).

3) Doubting dread is the most misleading of all: it comes from the father of lies, the infernal enemy. Hence, it can masquerade as meekness of heart. It arises to block us when we begin to hate sin and amend our lives. ("How can the all-perfect God continue to love me in my wretchedness, in my history of bad choices, in my immersion in the ways of evil?") Unable to cope with our sinfulness, we doubt the very goodness of God. But it is the work of Mother Jesus to turn any evil into good; and hence in this case the bitterness of doubt is transformed into the sweetness of love. Recalling that Christ is "the ground of our beseeching", she assures us that thus our doubting dread is overcome (LT 42). Specifying how we should pray in times of doubt, she recommends a short exercise of prayer designed to overcome doubting dread and to lead one to believe in the sweet goodness of God. In this exercise we thankfully bring before our eyes all that God has done—one gracious gift and action after another—assuring ourselves that if we alone existed, God would still have done all those things (LT 65). Such is the measureless goodness we contemplate after emerging from doubting dread.

## More on Reverent Dread

After the direct exposition of the faulty forms of dread Julian returns here and there in the text to deepen our understanding of reverent dread—the only kind which fully pleases God (LT 74). "All dreads, except reverent dread—though they may look holy—are not so true" (LT 74).

*Inseparable But Distinct*: Love and dread are children of the same divine goodness, being related both to the lordship of God and to God's goodness, which has earlier been identified with the motherhood. Both are gifts of grace; both are rooted likewise in nature (LT 74). Inseparable, one cannot exist without the other. We are unable to have one without the other: for the one who loves, also fears, regardless of any feelings. Yet love and fear are nonetheless distinct (LT 74).

*Effects:* Reverent dread is mild, and its bitterness is modified because of the concurrent presence of the sweetness of love. Both sentiments last into eternity, manifested here and forever as a love which is intimate and familiar, along with a fear which is reverential and courteous (LT 74). They are the basis of our trust. In the absence of fear, and of meek love, trust also falters.

It is with dread—with fear and uncertainty—that Julian desires at one time to know the extent and measure of her own sin—but she received no answer (LT 79). Even without such terrifying knowledge, she learns to be fearful because of her own inconstancy (LT 79).

At judgement fear will take hold of us as we see the cause of all that God has done: there will be fear—trembling and quaking—for joy (LT 75). Affirming what has been said about all creation, she tells us that: "All creatures shall have such reverent dread—surpassing all that has been felt before—until the pillars of heaven shall tremble and quake ... all without pain ..." (LT 75).[3] Reverent dread will reach a pinnacle at the end of time, when we shall actually see the reason God has done all that has been done. In the company of "all creatures", when the foundations of the earth are shaken, we shall tremble with awe (LT 75).

Fear does not dilute joy, for in heaven God shall be known and feared more intensely even than now (LT 75).

## Summary

From her own experience, and from her counselling of many persons who laid bare their fears to her, Julian offers a wise summation: "God showed me no souls except those who feared him" (LT 76). "The one who loves also fears" (LT 74).

Speaking with those whom she counselled, and to all others moved by fear across the ages, she offers this firm guidance: Let us desire of God to fear him reverently, to love him meekly, to trust him powerfully. We need to pray to our Lord of grace for the gift of reverent dread and meek love, in heart and deed. Without this no one can please God (LT 74). Such is the way to trust.

## Endnotes

1. For a brief but excellent overview of this theme, see Brant Pelphrey, *Love Was His Meaning: The Theology and Mysticism of Julian of Norwich* (Salzburg: Institüt für Anglistik und Amerikanistik, Universität Salzburg, 1982) 281–285. See also Bradley, "Julian's 'doubtfull drede'," *The Month* 243 (Feb., 1981): 53–57.

2. The Sloane text reads: "and thus this drede helpith us to seken comfort and mercy of God; and abileth us to have contrition be the blisfull touching of the Holy Gost". The Short Text includes the phrase *as ane antre* (Beer 78). Likewise, the Paris text, which Colledge and Walsh follow, reads: "and thus this drede helpys hym *as an antre*, etc." They translate this to say: "and so this fear helps him as though by chance ...." (*Julian of Norwich: Showings* 168). Yet their note from Hilton, *Scale II*, chap. 19 has the sense of a gate or entrance (*A Book of Showings* II, 672, note to l. 11) and is so translated by Clark and Dorward: "consider these as an entrance and a way" (with reference to religious practices). (Clark and Dorward 222). Beer cites such a meaning for *antre* from OED: "a means or way of entrance" (p. 97). This meaning seems consistent with the context in which Julian uses it.

3. She echoes here the Book of Job: "He shakes the earth out of its place,/and the pillars beneath it tremble" (9:6).

# THE WAY OF LONGING AND DESIRE

'This *desire* leads us on the right way ...'

Desire as a component of life in Christ has long been a theme of spiritual writers.[1] A text in Augustine concisely expresses the reciprocal role of desire in contemplative prayer, on the part of God and the soul: "I call you [my God] into my soul which you are making ready to receive you by the longing which you yourself inspire."[2]

Especially familiar to those in consecrated states of life were the words of the psalmist protesting that the desire for God is so great that it obliterates the desire for other delights:

Whom else have I in heaven?

And when I am with you, the earth delights me not.
                                        (Ps. 73:25).

Walter Hilton, in a chapter citing this scriptural text,
exclaims:

> Certainly, I would rather feel and have a true desire
> and a pure longing in my heart for my Lord Jesus, even
> though I should see nothing of him at all with my
> spiritual eye, than have without this desire ... all the
> joys of heaven and earth which I could have without
> this desire toward my Lord Jesus.[3]

But Julian's treatment is more comprehensive, basic, and
dynamic than what is commonly found. Like her understanding of compassion, her experience of desire expands. She
moves from a focus on herself, to Christ, and to the whole
Christ now growing into the new person. Thus we learn
what and how we are to desire in order to travel the right
way and become one with God.


## Her Individual Desires

When Julian tells us what she herself desired, she intermingles
counsel about the working of desire in any person who loves
God.

Though she was a little unsure about her desires for the
sickness and the vision, because they were out of the ordinary,
she knew that she was right in petitioning for the wounds,
which included a desire to suffer with Christ, and culminated
in an intentional longing for God.

In the first showing she actively desires to see even more,
especially of the "spiritual sight", which was that of Christ
in union with the Trinity. And from this beginning she yearns

to share this same sight with all her even-Christians so that it can be a comfort to them (LT 8). Again, speaking generally, she affirms that our deepest natural desire is to have God:

> For this is the natural *yearning* of the soul, by the touching of the Holy Ghost ... "God, in your goodness, give me yourself, for you are enough for me; and if I ask anything that is less, still will I be wanting, for only in you I have all" (LT 5).

We can never cease willing and longing until we have God in the fullness of glory (LT 6). This natural desire of our soul is so great that we would not be content if we had all things without God, even in the realm of the mind (LT 72). For example, there is great satisfaction in the intellectual understanding of our need for God, because we are fickle and foolish, and beset with sorrows and pain; but this insight is low and trivial when compared with "the great *desire* of the soul for God" (LT 47).

That such a longing is natural does not excuse us, however, from the need to desire and pray to remain in God's grace unto life's end (LT 33). Then we shall see clearly in him "all that we *desire*" (LT 47).

Probing beyond this principle, Julian examines the living dynamics of the desire for God. The least sight of him stirs us to seek for more, and when he discloses himself, we indeed have what we desire. The more we see him the more we desire him by grace (LT 43). She draws on echoes of the Song of Songs to express this: I saw him, sought him, possessed him, and wanted him (LT 10). Undeterred by distracting, unwanted desires of the flesh, though she knows they are not sin, she counsels herself and us to keep our intent and will stably set on being one with Jesus (LT 19). If we do not know how to seek God, "*desire* it of our Lord and he will teach us", for to be desired pleases and honours him (LT 77). Whenever we desire what we actually need, "God follows us, helping our *desire*" (LT 43). Seemingly she did not really need to see Mary in the flesh, for, as we have seen, her intense and persistent longing for this showing was not granted (LT 25).

In particular, what should we desire of Christ? First, "to dread, to love, and to trust" (LT 72). Further, we should all long for the grace to take joy in our redemption (LT 23)—indeed, to have spiritual delight in it (LT 23).

Her own spiritual delight, in the twelfth showing, is so great that it "surpasses all that the heart can will and the soul *desire*." The glorified Christ identifies himself in that showing as "he whom you *desire*" (LT 26). And in another place: "I am the one who places desire in your heart, and I am the fulfilment of all true desires" (LT 59). This experience of seeing and feeling the presence of God in this life "is greatly to be *desired*". For such an experience produces certainty about faith and firm hope, and is sweet and delightful (LT 65).

Seeing God's goodly and purposeful activity in all things further enkindles desire: "Then we can do no more than behold him, with joy, and with a sublime, powerful *desire* to be completely made one with him, centred in his dwelling place, enjoying his love and delighting in his goodness" (LT 43).

One desire, however, was greater than she could explain: it was not always with her, but left her and came back at the beginning of the thirteenth showing (LT 27). It was to remain till the end, she says. It concerned the reconciling of the two judgments on sin: our need for penitence, along with the absence of blame in God (LT 45). What this amounted to, of course, was the desire, which must remain unfulfilled in this life, of grasping the relation between time and eternity. For God loves us as we shall be when we are fulfilled, whereas we must stand before God as we are now.

It was not Julian's ambition to solve such a divine paradox intellectually. Rather, she longed to be assured that the one she most desired to love did not look on her with wrath and blame (LT 47). All of us must simply live with this troubling paradox like trusting children: we should desire really to grasp that our soul is united to God, unchangeable goodness (LT 46); and at the same time, seek forgiveness in God with a mighty desire for our salvation (LT 49). "And I saw with great clarity that it is imperative for us to keep ourselves in longing, and in penitence, until we are led so deep into God that we really and truly know our own soul" (LT 56).

We must face the fact, however, that we cannot fully know our real self until the final moment of life. We should therefore desire this final moment—not to hasten it, but to look forward to it: "to long and *desire* with all our strength to know ourself in the fullness of eternal joy" (LT 46). For her part, in the midst of her perplexity Julian addresses herself passionately to God as her maker "in whom I *desired* to see all truths" (LT 50). And mercifully the parable of the lord and the servant was given as a "misty" answer to her desire (LT 51). In that parable she gained assurance that God wants us to know the co-existence of the two truths that she found hard to reconcile—"insofar as it belongs to the creature" to know them (LT 50). When she was directed to mull over the details of the vision, she tells us: "I assented inwardly with great *desire*" (LT 51).

Julian's aggressive approach to God by fostering her natural desire is at odds with the widespread conception of the woman mystic as "passive". Rather, she resembles the bride in the Song of Songs who pursues her lover with passionate longing:

... I sought him/whom my heart loves/
I sought him but I did not find him./
... Have you seen him whom my heart loves?/
... [when] I found him whom my heart loves./
I took hold of him and would not let him go.

(Song of Songs 3:1-4).

Gregory of Nyssa, in his commentary on the Song, touches on this theme of "intentional longing for God" and also names it, as Julian and others do, a wound:

The soul, having gone out at the word of her Beloved, looks for Him but does not find Him ..... In this way she is, in a certain sense, wounded and beaten because of the frustration of what she desires ... every fulfilment of her desire continually generates further desire for the Transcendent ... she has received within her God's special dart, she has been wounded in the heart by the point of faith, she has been mortally wounded by the arrow of love. And *God is love.*[4]

Elsewhere, Gregory identifies the vision of God with desire:

... what Moses yearned for is satisfied by the very things which leave his desire unsatisfied ... for this truly is the vision of God: never to be satisfied in the desire to see him. But one must always, by looking at what he can see, rekindle his desire to see more.[5]

### Desire and the Thirst for God
### *"How Long Shall I Desire?"*

In the first showing Julian perceived that "our lover truly *desires* that we cling fast to him with all our strength and evermore cleave to his goodness" (LT 6). In the eighth show-ing she reports that the love Christ has for us was so strong that he chose his passion: "willfully and with great *desire*" (LT 20). In the ninth showing she pictures Christ as a glad giver, who *desires* only to please and solace those who receive his gifts (LT 23).

But it was in contemplating the parable of the lord and the servant that Julian learned more fully of the desire which burns in the heart of God, symbolized under the image of thirst. Desire in God is as real as the property of compassion and pity, and it will endure until the end of time (LT 31).

It is the same desire and thirst that Christ experienced on the cross and had from the beginning. It is no ordinary desire, but an intense "love-longing", which wants to have us all within him, made one with him, for his joy (LT 31, 40). In the midst of our pain, he is ever in our soul, loving us and longing to bring us to bliss (LT 51). This love-longing, which shall last until doomsday, was shown to Julian in con-junction with the motherhood of Christ. It is a longing he will experience "until all his precious children are born and brought forth" (LT 63). Hence, until we are born to the new life of the resurrection, we are enclosed in him. But great as is his longing for us, his wisdom and truth deter him from permitting the end to come until the best time (LT 31).

Even before she could distinguish the first Adam from the Christ Adam in the parable, Julian perceived that only his good will "and great *desire*" was the cause of his falling (LT 51). When she realized that the servant was Christ, God and man, she presents this desire again, in words passionate with longing:

And thus I saw the Son standing, saying, in effect:

194

"Lo, my dear Father, I stand before you in Adam's old
garment, ready to start off and to run.
"*I desire* to be on the earth for your glory, when it
is your will to send me.
*How long shall I desire?* (LT 51).

The Son, as eternal Wisdom, knew, of course, the time when
the Incarnation would take place, she explains. Therefore
this desire is that of the manhood of Christ. By this she
means the whole Christ: "for all mankind that shall be saved
by the sweet Incarnation and blissful passion of Christ—all
is the manhood of Christ; for he is the head, and we are
the members" (LT 51). This suggests the desire of the
nations for the Messiah, as expressed by the psalmist and
prophets. All the children of salvation are the manhood of
Christ.

This Christ-body is still in longing for the day "when every
woe and sorrow shall have an end, and everlasting bliss and
joy shall be fulfilled". Even the company of heaven longs
to see this day (LT 51).

## Longing for God and Longing with God

Once we have been taught by Julian what the desires are
that live in the heart of God, our own desires can be reformed
and enlarged. God's desires should be ours, too: a desire coming from the same divine power and looking toward the same
end.

Christ's desires correspond to our longings, but are infinitely
more inclusive and expansive: He wants us to be as much
at home with him "as mind may think or heart *desire*" (LT
77). Dwelling within us he wants us to be his helpers, and

195

to desire that all should be done that he is doing (LT 57). He wants us to know that, after a time of pain, we shall see in him all that we desire (LT 47)—in fact, that our recompense and reward, through the Spirit, will endlessly surpass all that we desire (LT 58). He longs for us "to *desire* with all our heart and all our strength" to have a knowledge of the Trinity, as one goodness, through its properties of kind (meaning both natural yearning and compassion), mercy, and grace (LT 56).

In the sixteenth revelation, which summed up all that went before, Julian arrives at a threefold enumeration of the divine desires which should be ours, too: 1) God desires to teach us to know and love him forever; 2) he longs to have us with him, and to be with those who are taken out of pain and drawn into heaven; and 3) he thirsts for that day when he will fulfil us all in bliss, an action reserved for the end of time (LT 75). The totality of God's desire is to have all humanity within himself. He has already drawn the blessed into himself; and he is now drawing his living members, too—and by the same power and for the same reason.

It is our duty to try to live "in sweet prayer and lovely *longing*" with our Lord Jesus (LT 40). In fact, the very definition of prayer includes the component of true desire (LT 42). When we are living in such prayer and love-longing, his blissful, lovely demeanour towards us is "glad and merry and sweet" (LT 71). When our courteous Lord shows himself thus to our souls, "we have what we *desire*"; and the more we see of God the more we desire him by grace (LT 43). Indeed, if we saw God continually the desire for him would utterly block out "any mischievous feeling or any yearning for sin" (LT 47).

Even though God is already unspeakably close to us, yet

we can never stop weeping (spiritually) and longing until we see God as the face of joy:

> God wants us *to long for*
> and *desire*
> this day of fulfilment (LT 56).

This desire "leads us on the right way." It "keeps us in true life and makes us one with God" (LT 75). Indeed, longing in God is indispensable for us, for it is none other but God's love drawing us into heaven (LT 75).

The theme of desire, in God and in us, occurs to the very end of her text. Regarding herself, as the recipient of the showings, she says: "I *desired* oftentimes to know what was our Lord's meaning" (LT 86). In reference to God, "his love makes him *to long*", as his wisdom, truth, and righteousness make him faithful to us here (LT 81). With regard to herself and her even-Christians:

> And by the great *desire* that I have in our blessed Lord
> that we live in this manner—that is to say, in *longing*
> and in enjoying, as the whole of this lesson of love
> shows—I understood thereby that all that is contrary
> to us is not from him but from our enemy. And he
> wants us to know this, by the sweet gracious light of
> his kind love (LT 82).

## Endnotes

1. See, for example, Walter Hilton, *The Scale of Perfection*, trans. John P.H. Clark and Rosemary Dorward (New York, Paulist Press, 1991), esp. Bk. 2, chaps. 41, 46.
2. *Confessions*, Bk. 13, chap. 1.
3. *The Scale of Perfection*, Bk. 1, chap. 47, 120.

4. *Commentary on the Song*, III:1037, as quoted in Andrew Louth, *The Origins of the Christian Mystical Tradition* (Oxford, Clarendon Press, 1981) 89.
5. *The Life of Moses*, Bk. Two, 239. Quoted in *Light from Light: An Anthology of Christian Mysticism*, ed. Louis Dupré and James A. Wiseman, O.S.B. (New York, Paulist Press, 1988) 57.

# V

# UNDERSTANDING HUMANITY'S PILGRIMAGE

## THE RIFT IN OUR BEING

### *Substance and Sensuality*

Desire is our way of union in this life; love, in its fullness, in the next. Between one state and the other lies the condition of brokenness within our nature, between our substance and sensuality.

Substance is sometimes taken, without qualification, as soul. Sensuality is sometimes read as the activities of the senses, or even as centred in carnality.[1]

Yet some of Julian's first editors supplied us with quite clear explanations of these terms. As early as 1877, Henry Collins, who is, in turn, quoted by Roger Hudleston (1927, 1952), wrote:

> By the word *substance* is to be understood the soul, considered in its *spiritual* nature and higher faculties. By the *sensuality* is meant the soul as knit to a *fleshly* nature, and affected by it. The *substance* or spirit is joined to Christ by the tie of fatherhood, because he, as God, created it. The *sensuality or flesh*, transmitted by Adam, became united to him when he, the Word, became incarnate. This union is handed on to the members of his Church by Baptism and the Holy

199

Eucharist. Christ thus knits to him the whole man—the
*spirit and the fleshly nature*, the *substance and the
sensuality.*[2]

This explanation falls short of making clear the connection
of the motherhood metaphor with the meaning of substance
and sensuality. But it faithfully transmits the important image
of "knitting", as connected with the other italicized terms.

We shall look first into what Julian means by substance
and sensuality; then, second, at the context in which her
image is created and shaped to her purposes; and lastly, we
shall consider the comprehensive treatment she gives to substance and sensuality through this image.

## *"We Are Double": Substance and Sensuality*

Julian describes our nature or kind as made up of substance
and sensuality, which are knit together and fastened to God.
The higher part is the key-point where we are open to the
Transcendent. When Julian says it is hard to know ourselves,
she is acknowledging the difficulty of knowing our substantial
soul: of understanding and experiencing ourselves as open
to the Divine Mystery—of being drawn to the Mystery
beyond our limited selfhood.

The lower part of our nature—our sensuality (body, and
soul in one sense)—is grounded in divine Wisdom made flesh,
in Christ Jesus. She uses the word soul to mean (1) soul in
the ordinary sense, as the animating principle affected by,
and affecting, the body; and (2) as substance: "Our substance
and sensuality can both be called our 'soul' because they are
united in God" [LT 56]).

By the sensual soul, the body realizes some of its potential in the physical order—memory, imagination, feeling, thought, emotions. We know that imagination, for example, can transport us where the body is not; and memory can restore to us what the body is no longer experiencing. In an intense transport or ecstasy in the natural order the soul may feel that it is all spirit, with the body either left behind or converted to spirit. Yet the mind knows better. Or the mind, by fear or apprehension, for example, can lay a burden on the body.

If we come to know the substantial soul, we become aware of the potential for being made one with the unlimited, compassionate, loving, eternal divine Mystery. In this point where we meet the transcendent, we are made so noble and rich, that always we carry out his will and give him worship. In contemporary terms the word substance bears some analogy to the "deep self" or the unconscious in the psychology of Carl Jung, though it is clearly not the same reality. In some sense the "deep self" is the presence of God within us.

But this does not detract from the dignity of our sensuality: for it is described as "the splendid city where our Lord Jesus takes his seat ... [and] in which he is enclosed" (LT 56).

But that is the way things are destined to become. At present, "In our substance we are full, and in our sensuality we fall short" (LT 57). In the area of sensuality, we encounter limits and failure and a falling short of what our heart desires. In time God will restore the defects in our sensuality, fulfilling it by the working of mercy and grace "plentifully flowing into us by his very godhead" (LT 57). When our sensuality, by the power of Christ's passion, will be brought up to the substance—having profited by the pain that is transformed by mercy and grace—we will have our increase and our fulfilment in Christ.

To give us a better notion of these involved concepts Julian uses the knitting image, in conjunction with the abstract term of "oneing", or uniting. "Union" does not adequately stand for what she means, because she is pointing both to a state of being and to a state of becoming, a twofold reality which the medieval word "oneing" can accommodate, but which the modern term "union" does not. Like others before her she speaks of this divine "oneing" in images.

## Context of the Image of Knitting

Conventional medieval metaphors of mystical union, both in art and in written texts, primarily focused on spousal imagery, highly sensual and often erotic, deriving from the Song of Songs.[3] The chief limitation of this imagery of union is that it is frequently restricted to the experience of the individual soul as the spouse of Christ as a bridegroom. But Julian employs imagery of union, not only to signify union with Christ by desire in this life and face-to-face love with him in heaven, but also uniting and union with our even-Christians in charity. For this purpose the image of knitting is apt. It means at a literal level to fasten securely. It may even draw on the craft of knitting: the producing of one fabric through the interlocking loops of a single thread of yarn.

Thus, knitting not only signifies unity but also connotes the activity of bringing about oneness. Julian is complex and versatile in her use of the image.

By contrast Walter Hilton, in *The Scale of Perfection*, uses the imagery of being intricately fastened to another on one level only: to encourage the devotion of the individual soul. He translates the passage in 1 John 4:3 to read: "Every Spirit that releases Jesus or unfastens him ... he is not from

God."[4] He specifies this image as knitting, in the sense of being firmly fastened to another:

> Jesus is *knitted and fastened* to a person's soul by a good
> will and a great desire for him. . . . The greater this
> desire, the more firmly is Jesus *knitted* to the soul; the
> less the desire, the more loosely is he *joined*. Then
> whatever spirit or feeling it is that lessens this desire
> . . . in order to set it upon itself, this spirit will *unknit*
> *and undo* Jesus from the soul; . . . if a spirit . . . increases
> this desire, *knots firmer the knot* of love and devotion
> to Jesus . . . this spirit is from God.[5]

It was common in theology to speak of the knitting of the divine and human natures of Christ into a unity which was one person.[6] Also literary precedent shows the use of "knitting" in the sense of the bones being knit together to form one body.[7] This is the sense of the image as used in the Pauline writings to speak of the mystical body: Christ and his members.[8]

Knitting imagery finds a place in medieval art and poetry also. In his comprehensive study of the miniatures of the *Rothschild Canticles*, Jeffrey Hamburger discusses the uses of such imagery to signify the Trinity. Both in the miniatures of the *Canticles* and in some Middle High German devotional poetry, the imagery of knots and weaving "expresses the unity and inseparability of the Persons":[9]

> The anonymous author of the *Granum sinapis* (or
> Eckhart himself, if he in fact is the author) opens the
> stanza describing the unity of the three Persons with
> the phrase, *Der Drier strik*, the threefold braid (or
> chain). According to the contemporary Latin

commentary, the phrase refers to the unity of the Persons.[10]

The images were also employed to suggest the inner life of the Triune God:

> In their efforts to describe the *perichorese*, "interpenetration" (literally, dancing around or rotation), of the three Persons, other German poets employed the images of knotting and weaving, for example, the verbs *stricken* (to knit, knot, or tie), *weben* (to weave), *dringen* (to twist, bind, wreath, or plait), or *velzen* (to fold, interlace, or intertwine).[11]

The poets worked out many variations on the same theme:

> The Trinity is variously described as "three heavenly youths [or heroes] woven into a single cloth [or chain]"; or "three persons braided and pressed into a single chain [or unity]." Another poem explains that "where the two are, there is the third [Person] knitted to them both."[12]

Despite these many precedents, Julian's imagery is generally of another sort. True, she uses the knitting image in the biblical sense of the binding into one of Christ and his body, though she develops the idea in a way not explicitly in Scripture. But, significantly, she does not employ the knitting image in speaking of the inner life of the divine Trinity. Whether consciously, intuitively, or because she recognized its limitations, Julian leaves no hint of this form of Trinitarian image. Such a use could be misleading, because it does not unambiguously suggest oneness of substance and trinity of operations, as orthodox belief holds with regard to God. Julian's image of knitting suggests union without identity, where such a concept is at stake.

She is within the parameters of that image when she uses "oneing"—intertwining—in connection with substance and sensuality.

## *The Image of Knitting in Julian's Text*

In a comprehensive passage Julian sums up the relation of our substance and sensuality to God, and the role of Christ in re-uniting our two "kinds":

> For the higher part of our nature [our substance] is knit to God in its creation;
>
> And God is knit to the lower part of our nature [our sensuality] in Christ's taking of our flesh;
>
> And thus in Christ our two kinds [natures] are made one (LT 57).

Underlying this overall statement are related uses of knitting and intertwining.

First, she examines the knitting of the created soul of Christ to the Trinity. Of this she says that the most perfect substance is the soul of Christ (LT 53). This most blessed soul was knit to God in its creation, with a knot so subtle and strong that it is made one with God (LT 53). In consequence of this union, the Godhead gave strength to the manhood of Christ to suffer more in the passion than would have been otherwise possible (LT 20).

Second, the soul of Christ is knit to his own body in the maiden's womb (LT 57), associating such knitting with the bonds of motherhood.[13] In consequence, he is knit to the sensuality of all the children of salvation and becomes "perfect"—complete—man (LT 57, 58). Paralleling the unbreakable knot in heaven, this knitting, too, signifies that God's Son and the complete Adam cannot be separated (LT 51). With overtones of the knitting which signifies covenant and marriage, it is said that "in the knitting and in the uniting, he is our true spouse, and we his beloved wife and fair maiden" (LT 58).

And from the third perspective, the human being is also knit to God and to Christ. Our substance is knit to God in our creation (LT 57). He made us all at once (that is, in his foreseeing purpose, not in a pre-existing state), knitting us to himself (LT 58). "We are made by God and in the same moment knit to God" (LT 53). Our soul is so completely fastened to God by his goodness, that there is nothing between God and the soul (LT 46). This does not, however, indicate identity. When Julian is so united to God in mutual joy that she could not distinguish her substance from God's, she still knows they are different: "God is God, and our subtance is a creature in God" (LT 54).

In consequence of being knit to God in creation, the substantial soul is made noble and rich and inclined always to do the will of God (LT 57). It is this substantial soul that is so knit to the Godhead that it can never sin (LT 53, 58). And God, in turn, being so intertwined to the soul in love, through its knitting to Christ, can never be wrathful (LT 49). Yet the perfect knitting of the soul and God is only gradually achieved: "Until I am so fastened to him that there is really nothing between God and me", I can never have true bliss (LT 5).

The substantial soul is able to transmit to the body, within limits, some of its nobility and richness (LT 57): faith, along with other virtues, comes down from the substance into the sensuality (LT 54). It follows, then, that sensuality, of which bodiliness is an essential (LT 56), has the capacity to receive such ennobling.

Yet sensuality has become loosened from the higher part: we are severed from our true selves. True, these parts will never be torn completely asunder, because they are both grounded in God (LT 56). But it is only by the power of the passion that our sensuality is brought up to the substance (LT 56; 58). Hence, "Notwithstanding this perfect knitting and this endless uniting, yet the redemption is needful and profitable for us" (LT 53). We are destined through that passion to become a new being in which the substance can flow unimpeded into the transformed bodily life.

Conflating the cloth image with another form of knitting—that of the vine and its branches—[14]Julian describes us as being rooted in God through love (LT 56). But the "old root"—humanity deriving from Adam—has been truncated; and it is the work of Christ to raise up "the old root rightfully knit to him in creation" (LT 55). By Christ we are both kept and restored.

Knitting also applies to the healing of bodily injuries. It is the object of the passion to knit together again the broken bones and lacerated skin in our sensuality and to unite it to our substance (LT 58).

Given the "wonderful knitting" which joins the sensual soul to the body, not even the body can be left to destruction and death. Indeed, it was unquestionably necessary ("It behovith nedes to ben") that mankind be restored from physical death and from the death of sin (LT 55). It is consistent with the righteousness of God that this created company that will fill heaven be so knitted to God that they can never be separated (LT 53).

But Christ's mystical body, in which all his members are

207

knit, is not yet fully glorified nor taken out of pain (LT 31). In his eternal thirst for this to be achieved, Christ's activity is to make us holy: "I shall gather you and make you holy by binding you to me" (LT 28). One of our rewards is seeing for ourselves the gathering of all mankind to be saved into the blessed Trinity through Christ's being "knitted" to his body (LT 31). In virtue of this union the wounds and the scars and unravelling of sins will be rewoven into a more beautiful and stronger pattern than if sin had not been.

And in this healing and restoring through Christ, we, too have a role: it is prayer. We are to live with all our intent and will set unwaveringly on the goal of the uniting of all in the Lord Jesus (LT 19). The fruit of prayer is to be brought indeed into oneness with Christ, and to become like him in all things (LT 42).

The experience of this uniting to God may at times be anticipated in this life when, with the suddenness of a divine touch, the soul is made one with God, when it is truly at peace with itself (LT 49).

We have an analogy of what Julian means by "touch" in our phrasing of being "touched" by the grief or by the generous actions of another. It is an experience by which we both feel and understand. Hence, Julian associates reason with this touch—a reason grounded in nature and in God; and she likewise associates understanding with desire in the same passage (LT 56).

Further, we may be able to commune, delightedly, with our own soul—that innermost life which is our substantial soul, strong in its oneness with God (LT 56).

Where shall we seek for that soul? Only in God, wherein it is rooted in endless love—knit to God like branches knotted to the tree.

## In Summary

Julian is quite at odds with medieval thinking which generally saw the soul and body as fully separate, with the body always impeding the soul. Julian, as we have seen, thinks of one soul, knitted to God in the higher part, and knitted to the body, in union with Christ, in the lower part. By making only this basic distinction within the human being, and by stressing that Christ assumed our total sensuality, Julian also bypasses the allegorizing of contemplative and active powers of reason and passion which was derogatory to the woman. In that tradition the higher powers of reason represented the male, and the lower powers of appetite stood for the instability of the woman. But for Julian, reason is "grounded in kind," while being at the same time in marvellous accord with the high part (LT 83). The only mastery Julian presents is that of the inward part (the substantial soul) over the outward part (LT 19), and these are not labelled as representing gender. She stresses overall that Christ gave dignity to our entire, individual humanness, in which resides a natural desire for God; and to our humanity corporatively, out of the diversities of which is unfolding the glorious city that is to come.

## Endnotes

1. Brendan Doyle, for example, identifies "sensuality" in Julian with that in romantic tales of the Middle Ages: the Grail legends, Percival, Tristan, and Isolde: "Julian's images are images found in these tales—'longing', 'desire', 'thirst', 'compassion', 'sensuality'." *Meditations with Julian of Norwich* (Santa Fe., N.M., Bear and Company, 1983) 18. This is hardly consistent with

the author's explanation later, of sensuality as "the miracle of the Incarnation through which we are oned to the Trinity". p. 19. Actually, Julian says that by the Incarnation, God is made one with us (see below).

2. *Revelations of Divine Love Shewed to a Devout Ankress by Name Julian of Norwich*, ed. Dom Roger Hudleston, O.S.B. (London, Burns Oates, 1952) 175.

3. See "The Mystical Union Miniatures", in Jeffrey F. Hamburger, *The Rothschild Canticles* (New Haven and London, Yale University Press, 1990) 105–117.

4. Walter Hilton, *The Scale of Perfection*, Bk. I, chap. 12, trans. John P.H. Clark and Rosemary Dorward (New York, Paulist Press, 1991) 85: ("What knittith Ihesu to mannes soule" (I.12.8a).

5. *Scale*, Bk. I, chap. 12, 86.

6. See also MED *knitten*: ca.1400, *Cursor Mundi* 18812: "Monhede but erthe what is hit That now with the godhede is *knyt*?"

7. See MED, *knitten*, 6, ca. 1440—Lord gode Ihu 6: 'My body, swa made of vile matere, Thow *knyttide* to-gedire in Ioyntes sere"; and ca. 1475, *Ms. Welcome Foundation Library* 564, 13a/b: "The bonys were *knittid* togideris for it is resonable that they be *knytt togideris* that many bonys myghten make oon body."

8. MED, *knitten* 6. ca. 1400. Pauline Epistle Eph. 4,16: "Alle the body is maad to gydere and *knyt* [L.connexum] to gydre." Also, 1425, Wyclif Sermons 9:27: "The secounde oonheede is of man, that many partis of him ben *knitt* in oo soule.'

9. Jeffrey F. Hamburger, *The Rothschild Canticles* Art and Mysticism in Flanders and the Rhineland Circa 1300 (New Haven and London, Yale University Press, 1990) 139.

10. Hamburger 139.

11. Hamburger 139.

12. Hamburger 139.

13. See Psalm 139:13: "Truly you have formed my inmost being\ you knit me in my mother's womb."

14. MED, *knotte*, 5: ca. 1398. John de Trevisa, trans. Bartholomew de Glanville's *De Proprietatibus Rerum* 208b/a: "Everich tree,

herbe, and grass hath a roote, and in the roote many maner knottes and strynges ... And knottes and strynges beth in the stede of sinewes and byndeth togideres the partyes."

## "SIN IS BEHOVABIL"

Why was sin allowed? And why was its consequence, pain, allowed? These vexing, all-important questions relate to our salvation, for if we do not understand them, we could be led into despair. If we do understand them, we have a source of great comfort in the sorrows of this present life. The eighth and the thirteenth showings in particular deal with these matters: (1) What is the reason for pain? (2) How can it be said that sin, which causes pain, is the right way—"behovabil"? and (3) What are the "great deeds" that bring about the overcoming of sin and pain?

### The Reason for Pain

Out of the depths of her compassion Julian asks first why Christ suffered. "The reason Christ suffered is that he wants, out of his goodness, to make us higher with him in bliss" (LT 21). Furthermore, the suffering of Christ, the innocent one, highlights the role of patience in transforming the world and giving victory to humanity.[1]

And why do we suffer? So that we can see with our interior sight. We will come to see what the not-good, or, better, the noughting of good, is. We will come to know our self, and what we are of our ego-self without God. We will ask mercy. This is why even undeserved pain is profitable: sometimes we are simply left to ourselves better to learn our need for God (LT 15). Such was Julian's experience.

In her reflections on sin, and the pain it causes, Julian, as in other situations, was "in part fulfilled with compassion" for all her even-Christians (LT 28). This was followed by comfort which she could extend to others: "For this little pain that we suffer here we will have a high, endless knowing of God which otherwise we should never have had" (LT 21).

Christ continues to suffer in us, so that we can rise in him:

I understood that we are now, as our Lord sees it, on his cross with him in our pains and our passion, dying; and if we deliberately remain with him on that same cross with his help and his grace unto the end, suddenly he will change his demeanour towards us, and we shall be with him in heaven (LT 21).

To every sin there is a corresponding pain. This is not because God is vengeful, but because God is truth. And to every sin there corresponds a new degree of bliss, because God is love (LT 38).

## But Why Was Sin Allowed?

This justifies God as truth and love. But the underlying question is still unanswered: Since God is all-wisdom, why was sin allowed in the first place? (LT 27). God assures Julian that it is precisely because of his wisdom that sin is allowed: in view of what God ordains for us, sin is "behovabil": rightly ordained. It needs must be. It is the way to a greater good, to the ultimate working out of divine purposes. Sin reveals God more fully as wisdom and goodness, which means Jesus

Christ as mother. This goodness is the property in God which does good against evil, "and thus Jesus Christ who does good against evil is our true mother" (LT 59). As one medieval text has it, Christ is the hewn-rock from which the life-giving waters abound.[2] Similarly from the breasts of Mother Christ flow the food and drink of life in the sacraments.

In the fourteenth showing, after the parable of the lord and the servant and after the reflections on Christ as mother, Julian repeats and expands her answer to why sin has been allowed:

> All this bliss we have by mercy and grace. This manner
> of bliss we should never have known if the properties
> of goodness, which is God, had not been opposed,
> whereby we have this bliss (LT 59).

There are three stages to this transformation of evil into a greater good:

> [1] Wickedness has been allowed to rise in opposition
> to goodness, [2] and the goodness of mercy and grace
> then opposed the wickedness, [3] and turned all to
> goodness and to the honour of those who will be saved
> (LT 59).

Essentially this process is the transforming of sin into love, through patience in suffering, which is love's "supreme expression".[3] Sin was allowed ("suffered") to set the scene for God's "sufferance" (his patient endurance of pain) (LT 27, 35). As a recent writer summarizes:

> ... the very purpose of sin is to evoke this "sufferance"
> from Jesus, so that He may express His love by suffering

213

the pain that saves mankind, and so teach mankind its
utter dependence upon Him."[4]

It is humanity's part to see suffering, not as vengeful divine
punishment for sin, but as the occasion for transforming the
sinful human condition, in ourselves and in others, into relationships of love.

## The Three Great Deeds

This pattern of transformation is worked out by the examples
of the three great deeds, all of which are part of the overcoming of sin and its devastation.

What we are to know about these great deeds is circum-
scribed by the principles that govern our knowledge of divine
mysteries. This applies in particular to Julian's plaintive objection, repeated reverently to God: "Lord, how can everything
be well, considering the great harm that has come through
sin to your creatures?" (LT 29).

We can indeed know God in part. Some truths are open,
clear, full of light, and abundant. All those of good will can
know them (she does not here exclude non-Christians). These
truths are taught, of course, outwardly by the church, but
also inwardly by the Holy Spirit (LT 30). No limits are set
on seeking such knowledge.

There are other truths about God, hidden and concealed
from us, and not relevant to our salvation. We are servants.
God rules a kingdom. It is not for us to know these secrets
God does not see fit to disclose. The more we try to probe
into them, the further we are from truly knowing them (LT
30, 33). This, no doubt, would include also those who try
to exploit mystical experiences for their own sake, attempting

to seize mystical joys by force and by the power of their own techniques.

These guidelines indicate what we can know about the three great deeds which make all things well.

(1) One deed is the work of Christ from the Incarnation to the Resurrection (LT 23). The purpose of this deed was advanced, and in no way thwarted, by the evil intentions of his persecutors. It culminated in the rising of the crucified one, and hence in the overcoming of death. Christ himself could then ask: "Was it not necessary that the Messiah should suffer these things and enter into his glory?" (Luke 24, 26)

It was a perfect work: "This deed and this work concerning our salvation was ordained as well as God could ordain it ... Christ's bliss would not have been complete if it could have been done any better" (LT 22). Sin is needful in some mysterious way for Christ in order for him to be crowned in victory. One sign of that victory is that sins will not be shame for the redeemed but will be transformed into honour.

(2) There is a second great deed now being done which can be known in part (LT 36). It is a work done by the Lord God for humanity in general, without excluding the individual. Like the first deed, sin can not block it. It is not known openly, but it is disclosed in part to some of Christ's lovers. It will extend to the end of time, and will be "admirable, wonderful, and abundant" (LT 36). It is intended to fill us with joy. Yet, while rejoicing in it, Julian says it was not revealed to her what this deed will be. But she keeps the knowledge of it before her, wisely, faithfully, and trustfully. Clearly it has something to do with our salvation, with prolonging the work begun in Christ's life on earth.

(3) Lastly, there is the "great deed" to be done by the Trinity on the last day. Ordained from the beginning this deed will make all things well, thereby making good on God's

215

promise to bring greater good out of evil. It shall be known to no one—not even the saints in heaven—until the last day (LT 36). Again, no sin could destroy it.

We have only the first deed, which we know about, as a guide to what we can know about the second and third deeds. Respecting Julian's caution that we refrain from speculating on the nature of these deeds, we can still consider what they might be like. For we know what the first deed is like.

For one thing, a "deed", as Julian uses the term with reference to the life of Christ, does not designate a single event. It refers to an action with many parts, moving unerringly, by interlocking causes, to achieve God's purpose, somewhat like the "action" of a drama. Second, this first deed was so integrated into human life, especially in its ordinariness, that it required faith to perceive it for what it really was: the coming of the kingdom of God. We may expect the same of the succeeding deeds. In the third place the deed, which was the life of Christ, was threatened repeatedly by evil purposes which could not frustrate it but only add to its glory and success. So it shall be again.

## Non-Deeds and Naughting

In our blind judging we take as deeds what are merely nothings. A non-deed is like sewing in cloth without ever fastening the beginning point or the end point—that is, in Julian's words, knotting. (Without knotting, all movement is naughting.) Non-deeds are the way of those foolish members of the first Adam who are not united to the risen Christ who is Wisdom. Non-deeds have been portrayed dramatically in the lament of Shakespeare's Macbeth, who sees a meaningless life culminating in "the *way* to dusty death":

Tomorrow, and tomorrow and tomorrow
Creeps in this petty pace from day to day
To the last syllable of recorded time,
And all our yesterdays have lighted fools
The *way* to dusty death.


And further, a non-deed is *nothing* because it is energy without direction. It lacks meaning—like the jumbled, disordered ramblings of the demented:

> It is a tale
> told by an idiot, full of sound and fury,
> Signifying *nothing*. (*Macbeth*, act 5, scene 5)


It is a non-deed because it rises up to try to destroy love, goodness, and truth.

All that is fully good, God does it. God "suffers" all that is evil: puts up with it, and accepts the pain from it. Evil is not to be admired or gloried in, but God's sufferance of it is. All this is done so that his goodness will be known without end. Sin is therefore the right way for God's purposes. It helps reveal God as Mother Wisdom, who turns evil into good and transforms pain into joy. The blindness that is sin causes pain, which in turn heals our blindness and opens our interior eye. Pain is the symptom of illness which prompts us to seek a remedy and avert disaster.

But "naughting" is not a non-deed, though it is painful. Pain, whether or not it follows on sin, prepares for "naughting"— the emptying out of our selfish, sinful individuality, our undue sheltering of that in us which seeks satisfaction without regard to others. Paradoxically, we then become uniquely ourselves, freed of the counterfeit self that is inflated with false desires and illusions. "Naughting" is not a loss of identity, but an entering, liberated, into the whole.

In Christ "naughting" was the embracing of pain, even to despair, on the cross. Thereby he poured out his individuality on the larger self, the mystical body, and in the resurrection became the cosmic Christ.

But all of this is known only by faith. Part of the beatitude of heaven is to see for ourselves, Julian says, that sin is "behovabil" (LT 27).

## Endnotes

1. See Anna P. Baldwin, "The Triumph of Patience in Julian of Norwich and Langland", in *Langland, the Mystics and the Medieval Mystical Religious Tradition*, ed. Helen Phillips (Cambridge, D.S. Brewer, 1990) 71–83.
2. *Summa Virtutum de Remediis Animae*, ed. S.Wenzel, Chaucer Library (University of Georgia) 202. Cited by Baldwin 74.
3. Baldwin 75.
4. Baldwin 76.

## HOW "ALL THINGS SHALL BE WELL"

Our *way* and our heaven
   is *true love and unwavering trust.*
Concerning this, he gave understanding in all the
showings:
   —and especially in the showing of the passion
     where he made me powerfully to choose him
     for my fulfilment.

Let us flee to our Lord:
   and we shall be comforted.
Let us touch him:
   and we shall be made clean.
Let us cling to him:
   and we shall be safe and secure from all kinds of perils
                        (LT 77).

## *"Prepare the Way for the People"*

"Christ is our *way*, securely leading us by his laws" (LT 55). On earth as our mother—whose tenderness is without compare—"he kindles our understanding, *directs our ways*, soothes our conscience, comforts our souls, and gives us, in part, knowing and loving of his blessed Godhead" (LT 61). Having all of us who will be saved enclosed in himself, he gives birth to us anew in heaven (LT 55).

As long as we are in this changeable life, the Holy Ghost dwelling in our soul brings us the gift of peace and of mercy: This is the *way* in which our Lord continually leads us (LT 48). In this mortal life our *way* is mercy and forgiveness, leading us always to more grace (LT 50).

For all under heaven who will eventually come there, the *way* is by never-ending longing and hope, as was shown in the servant standing before the Lord (LT 51).

Pain and sorrow will be ended for all the dear, dear
people of God. In our fulfilling and our new life we
shall truly see the reason for all that God has done.
We shall marvel at the greatness of God, the maker,
and the infinitesimal littleness of all that is made. We
should desire this sight and behold it in wonder. For
this sight *leads us in the right way*, keeps us in true life,
and interweaves us with God (LT 75).

Always Julian reminds us this is the way for the people of God to enter the city of beatitude. Christ continues to thirst for this consummation (LT 75). Meantime, we are God's helpers. We find a similar theme in Isaiah:

> "Pass through, pass through the gates,
> *prepare the way* for the people;
>
> Build up, build up the *highway*,
> clear it of stones ...
>
> They shall be called the holy people,
> the redeemed of the LORD,
>
> And you shall be called ...
> a city that is not forsaken (Is. 62:10,12).

The highest good for all, whether they know it or not, "is the future of God's kingdom". And this kingdom is the future role of God in human affairs:

> If a particular action springs from the spirit of creative love and contributes to the individual and social integration, unity and peace, then that particular action expresses the spirit of God's Kingdom.
>
> In pursuing such actions, the life of the individual will be integrated into personal integrity through membership in a communion which is itself related to larger communities and is finally related to the whole of mankind ....
>
> He who despises the preliminary as in Jesus while he waits for the ultimate will not be able to recognize the ultimate in its coming.[1]

220

The community of humanity will be integral to the restoring of all that has been made:

Every kind of nature that he has caused to flow out
of himself

to fulfil his purposes

he will bring back and restore again in himself

*by making humanity whole*
through the working of grace (LT 62).

Thus is amplified the assurance from the third showing, with its affirming of the ongoing action of the divine Trinity: "See, I lead everything to the end I ordained it for from without beginning—by the same power, wisdom, and love by which I made it" (LT 11).

## In the Guise of a Child

Paradoxically humanity becomes whole in the guise of a child. Such is the meaning of the vision of the little child raised out of wretchedness into glory:

At this time I saw a body lying on the earth, heavy
and ugly, without shape and form, like a swollen heap
of foul mud. And suddenly out of this body sprang a
most comely creature, a little child perfectly shaped and
formed, active and lively, whiter than a lily, which
quickly glided into heaven. The bloatedness of the body
stands for the great wretchedness of our mortal flesh,
and the smallness of the child stands for the cleanness
and purity of the soul (LT 64).

This is Julian's self-image, at the point of her greatest pain and gravest temptation to impatience. She has just been longing "to be delivered from this world and from this life", with its pain and woe. She has been suffering intensely from the greatest pain: the absence of God. She is this child, malnourished and diseased externally, wanting to be delivered—set free from all this world's wretchedness. And Julian is all her even-Christians. For they, too, can fall back into "heaviness and spiritual blindness and the experience of pains of spirit and body" (LT 64).

But even now, in the symbol of a little child, there is a soul, both substantial and sensual, which is clean and undefiled. It is made for bliss and friendship, not for power; for love, not for domination—for lowliness is the highest stature:

> And I understood that there is no higher stature in this life than childhood, in feebleness and in failing of power and of intellect—unto the time that our gracious mother has brought us up to our father's bliss (LT 63).

This child will be taken from pain, with no threat of a return of sorrow: God promises "a complete deliverance" (LT 64). But not yet. Hard as it may be, we are counselled to take our painful waiting and our discomfort as lightly as we can: "to set them at nought". In the meantime, we are to take "his promises and his comforting" as inclusively as we can (LT 64).

This child is each one who has been wounded and healed of sin, as is indicated in a passage which anticipates and parallels the vision of the transformed child, with its theme of deliverance:

Then are they [those discouraged by sin] suddenly
*delivered* from sin and from pain and taken up into bliss
and even made great saints" (LT 39).

Three degrees of bliss are in store for each one, at the moment
of being "*delivered* from pain" in this life: recognition from
God (which is a kind of "thanking"); thanks and honouring
from all those in heaven; and the awareness that this bliss
is ever-new, and forever (LT 14). One thing God means by
"all shall be well" is that "the least thing shall not be forgotten" (LT 32).

Julian reflected over the years on God disclosed in the *passion*, in a *point*, and on *pilgrimage* with us (LT 81). But God's
*resting place*, where the Lord Jesus stays and reigns, is in the
vast city that is humanity, where all sit down in equality
as at a great feast. When the great deed is accomplished, we
shall see for ourselves how this is an ultimate revelation of love.

## At the Window of the Anchorhold[2]

In the sixteenth showing, which repeated, integrated, and
expanded all the rest, Julian continued to ask God how, in
actuality, all things could be well. Since this query is also
ours, we can vividly conjecture how insistently she continued
to press her question. It is as if we passed by her anchorhold
window and overheard a lovers' quarrel: a holy altercation
as in Job. We hear God's words and can supply Julian's speculatively.

Julian wants to know "how can all things ever be well?"

God cites an impressive record: "I made all things from
nothing in the first place." Sin, as we have seen, is really
"nothing". So I can make well all that is not well (LT 32).

Furthermore, "I have already made well that first and

greatest harm (the sin of Adam); and I want you to know thereby that I will make well all that is less" (LT 29).

But, Julian insists, this present situation requires the impossible to be made well.

God answers gently: "True, you cannot do the impossible. But I can. Hence, all things can be made well" (LT 32).

Even this assurance does not put Julian fully at ease. For the tribulations, then and to come, are horrible. They include pain, ravaging disease, violence, hunger, rejection, church schisms, separations, despair, death, the mystery of evil. And in the vision of the passion in some way Julian had seen all this suffering. Julian may well ask of Christ (in our name, too): "Really, what kind of mother are you?" with the candour possible only with those we love. All is not well: none of these things are being made right, are they?

To us God sounds defensive: "I didn't say that!"

A symbolic storm at sea takes shape in Julian's mind: with the winds lashing and the frail crew labouring against all odds. Such is the church and the world.

Still, to us, God sounds defensive:

"I did not say you would not be tempested.

"Nor did I say you would not be travailed."

"Then what did you say?"

God answers this time "sharply" and with a mighty voice: "What I said is that you will not be overcome!" (LT 68).

## What, Then, Is Julian's Way?

Only when the final judgements are in will we no longer be stirred to say in any way to the Lord: "Lord, if it had been thus and so, then all had been well" (LT 85). At the end we shall say in one mighty chorus: "Indeed, this is the way things are, and it is well." For we shall then see truly that "all things are done as it was ordained before anything was made" (LT 85).

Though tempested and travailed, we can have a "mighty" trust and lasting comfort. Why? Because God loves us and takes delight in us. And he wills that we—by nature and grace—love in return, and take delight in this one who loves. And then, all shall be well (LT 68). We are to love God, ourselves in God, and all that God loves, for God (LT 84).

> For Love has no beginning,
>   and this love is God;
> and Love has been created,
>   and is our soul in God;
> and Love is a gift enabling us to live with
>   contrition,
>   compassion,
>   and rightful desire.
> All this, God means by love.
> This, finally, is Julian's *way*.

## Endnotes

1. Wolfhart Pannenberg, *Theology and the Kingdom of God*, ed. Richard John Neuhaus (Philadelphia, Westminster Press, 1969), 118, 126.
2. The texts from Julian in this section are obviously imaginative, though based on the chapters cited in parenthesis.

# SELECTED BIBLIOGRAPHY

*Editions*:

Beer, Frances, ed. *Julian of Norwich's Revelations of Divine Love.* Heidelberg, Carl Winter, 1978. (Short Text, B.L. Add. MS 33790.)

Colledge, Edmund, and Walsh, James, eds. *A Book of Showings to the Anchoress Julian of Norwich.* 2 vols. Toronto, Pontifical Institute of Medieval Studies, 1978. (Critical edition; all known mss.)

Glasscoe, Marion, ed. *A Revelation of Love.* Exeter, Exeter University Press, 1989. (Long Text—B.L. Sloane MS 2499.)

Reynolds, Frances (Sister Anna Maria, C.P.), ed. *A Critical Edition of the Revelations of Julian of Norwich* (1342–ca. 1416). *Prepared from All Known Manuscripts.* Unpublished Ph.D. dissertation, 1956.


*Translations*:

Colledge, Edmund, and Walsh, James, eds. *Julian of Norwich Showings.* New York, Paulist Press, 1978. (Short and Long Texts, from critical edition.)

John-Julian, O.J.N, Rev. *A Lesson of Love.* London, Darton, Longman and Todd, 1988; New York, Walker, 1988. (Long Text, presented in sense lines, showing parallelism of the text.)

del Mastro, M.L., ed. *Revelations of Divine Love.* Garden City, N.Y., Doubleday and Company, Image Books, 1977. (Sloane MS 2499, with Sloane 3705 "as a corrective", and Paris Fonds Anglais MS 40.)

Wolters, Clifton, ed. *Revelations of Divine Love.* Baltimore, Md., Penguin Books, 1973. (From Sloane MS 2499.)


*Secondary Works*:

Baldwin, Anna P. "The Triumph of Patience in Julian of Norwich and Langland", *Langland, the Mystics and the Medieval English*

*Religious Tradition*, Essays in Honour of S.S. Hussey. Ed. Helen Phillips. Cambridge, D.S. Brewer, 1990. 71–84.

Bradley, Ritamary. "The Goodness of God: A Julian Study." *Langland, the Mystics and the Medieval English Religious Tradition*, 85–96.

"Metaphors of Cloth and Clothing in the *Showings* of Julian of Norwich", *Mediaevalia* 9 (1986 for 1983), 269–282.

Bynum, Caroline Walker. *Jesus as Mother*. Studies in the Spirituality of the High Middle Ages. Berkeley, CA, University of California Press, 1982.

Clark, J.P.H. "*Fiducia* in Julian of Norwich", *Downside Review* 99 (1981): I, 97–108; II, 214–229.

"Nature, Grace and the Trinity in Julian of Norwich." *Downside Review* 100 (July, 1982), 203–220.

Glasscoe, Marion. "Visions and Revisions: A Further Look at the Manuscripts of Julian of Norwich", *Studies in Bibliography*, Papers of the University of Virginia 42 (1989): 103–120.

Hanshell, D. "A Crux in the Interpretation of Dame Julian", *Downside Review* 92 (1974): 77–91.

Janda, James. *Julian: A Play Based on the Life of Julian of Norwich*. New York, The Seabury Press, 1984.

Llewelyn, Robert, ed. *Julian Woman of Our Day*. London, Darton, Longman and Todd, 1985; Mystic, Conn., Twenty-Third Publications, 1987.

Pelphrey, Brant. *Christ Our Mother. Julian of Norwich*. Wilmington, Del., Michael Glazier, 1989 (now Collegeville, Mn., Liturgical Press).

Upjohn, Sheila. *In Search of Julian of Norwich*. London, Darton, Longman and Todd, 1989.

# INDEX